0426000M

Miracle of
ISRAEL

The Shocking, Untold Story of God's Love for His People

Gary Frazier & Jim Fletcher

First printing: March 2016
Second printing: July 2016

Copyright © 2016 by Gary Frazier and Jim Fletcher. All rights reserved. No part of this book may be used or reproduced in any manner whatsoever without written permission of the publisher, except in the case of brief quotations in articles and reviews. For information write:

New Leaf Press, P.O. Box 726, Green Forest, AR 72638

New Leaf Press is a division of the New Leaf Publishing Group, Inc.

ISBN: 978-0-89221-740-3
Library of Congress Number: 2016930926

Cover by Diana Bogardus

Unless otherwise noted, Scripture quotations are from the King James Version (KJV) of the Bible.

Please consider requesting that a copy of this volume be purchased by your local library system.

Printed in the United States of America

Please visit our website for other great titles:
www.newleafpress.net

For information regarding author interviews,
please contact the publicity department at (870) 438-5288.

New Leaf Press
A Division of New Leaf Publishing Group
www.newleafpress.net

CONTENTS

A Word from Gary 9

Preface 13

Section One: The Past

Chapter 1 — Beginnings and Father Abraham 19

Chapter 2 — The Reign of Judges, Saul, David,
and Solomon 37

Chapter 3 — The Prophets 41

Section Two: The Present

Chapter 4 — The Jesus Years 55

Chapter 5 — Next Year in Jerusalem 63

Chapter 6 — The State of Israel Is Born 79

Chapter 7 — Israel Today 107

Section Three: The Future

Chapter 8 — God's Endgame 123

Chapter 9 — The Millennial Kingdom 135

Chapter 10 — Glory 139

Appendix I: Prophecies Fulfilled at the First Coming
of Christ 153

Appendix II: Israel's Declaration of Independence 157

Appendix III: Fulfillment of Biblical Prophecies 163

Appendix IV: Use of "Palestine" versus "Israel" 177

Appendix V: Understanding the Balfour Declaration 181

Appendix VI: The Time of Israel's Judgment 185

A Word from Gary

Have you ever experienced a miracle? How would you define a miracle? Would you recognize a miracle if in fact you witnessed it? On the surface, most people say no to the first question, stammer on the second, and hesitate to answer the last. Yet miracles do occur on a daily basis, and therefore we should be very careful before denying their existence. The first prime minister of Israel, David Ben-Gurion, is purported to have stated, "He who does not believe in miracles is not realistic." This is a remarkable statement from a man who lived his life as an atheist.

I want to be clear, I believe in miracles. I believe in miracles not just because I have both seen and experienced miracles in my journey, but primarily because I know God and His Word.

The book in your hand is a book about a miracle and subsequent miracles. The historical narrative we trace begins in Ur of the Chaldeans in Mesopotamia, moves to an ancient land known as Canaan, then to Egypt, continues to a cross in Jerusalem, and spreads to the many nations of our world before arriving at a barn in Austria. It then comes to a courtroom in Vienna, continues to a hotel in Switzerland, a house in Tel Aviv, the West Wing of the White House, and to presidential palaces in Cairo, Egypt; Amman, Jordan; and Damascus, Syria.

As we journey we will be introduced to men of faith, such as Abraham, Moses, King David, Solomon, and many others. You will meet men and women of vision such as Eliezer Ben Yehuda, Theodore Herzl, David Ben-Gurion, Golda Meir, and Menachem Begin. We will dig into the role played by former presidents of America and be amazed as we see God working through men in history to bring about the fulfillment of His Word.

This story recalls the horrors of the Holocaust, the struggle of a people to survive and ultimately flourish in a difficult and hostile land surrounded by enemies. It is a record of wars fought, ethnic clashes, and constant interference and pressures from foreign powers. This is a story of a people and a nation hated by most, tolerated by some, cherished by God, and loved by the followers of His Son, the Lord Jesus Christ.

This journey finally ends on the Mount of Olives in Jerusalem, having encompassed a time span of six thousand years. Our quest will take us back to the Garden of Eden in ancient Mesopotamia and forward to modern-day Israel and finally on to the New Jerusalem.

This is a book about miracles of history that affect each and every one of us, whether we recognize them or not. We will ponder how the Creator God has and is working in the history of His world. In the end we will see that God has done and will do exactly as He promised as recorded in Isaiah 46:9–10, where He states:

> Remember the former things of old: for I am God, and there is none else; I am God, and there is none like me. Declaring the end from the beginning, and from ancient times the things that are not yet done. saying, My counsel shall stand, and I will do all my pleasure.

The Creator God had a plan from the very beginning, and if we look for His hand in world history, both past and present, we can be certain of His hand in the future. Join me now as we journey down the corridors of time, along the halls of history and experience with me, *The Miracle of Israel: The Shocking, Untold Story of God's Love for His People.*

Gary D. Frazier
Jerusalem, Israel

Preface

In November of 2011 I received a life-altering call notifying us that my wife, Sandra, had inoperable, incurable breast cancer. After tests at MD Anderson Cancer Center in Houston, Texas, we were told she had 36 months to live, more or less. In March 2012, God healed her! Do you believe God can heal? The Bible, God's Word, teaches there are three types of illness.

1. A sickness unto chastisement

In other words, we have chosen to sin against God, to break His law, and as such we suffer the consequence of our rebellion. The Apostle Paul writes to the church in Corinth in 1 Corinthians 11:29–30 and states, "For he that eateth and drinketh unworthily, eateth and drinketh damnation to himself, not discerning the Lord's body. For this cause many are weak and sickly among you, and many sleep [die]."

2. A sickness unto death

Ecclesiastes 3:1–2 states, "To every thing there is a season, and a time to every purpose under the heaven: A time to be born, and a time to die." Hebrews 9:27 tells us, "It is appointed unto men once to die."

3. A sickness unto the glorification of God

> And as Jesus passed by, he saw a man which was
> blind from his birth. And his disciples asked him, saying,
> Master, who did sin, this man, or his parents, that he
> was born blind? Jesus answered, Neither hath this man
> sinned, nor his parents: but that the works of God should
> be made manifest in him (John 9:1–3).

So, we prayed and asked God if there was willful sin or disobedience that brought the cancer on. No! Was it Sandra's time to physically die? We felt the Lord God was not through with either of us, and we agreed. No! So we prayed and waited, and we like to call what happened *God's Miracle for Sandra*.

But the fact is, God is always at work keeping His promises IF we are paying attention.

The October War Miracle

It was October 1973 in the midst of the Yom Kippur War. Israel was defending its right to exist after being attacked by Egypt and Syria on their holiest day of the year, the Day of Atonement, *Yom Kippur* in Hebrew.

Investigative reporter Michael Greenspan recounts the following as seen in the made-for-TV series *Against All Odds* produced by William (Bill) McKay. A small company of IDF soldiers led by David Yanev was in northern Israel on the Golan Heights attempting to infiltrate into the Syrian village of Quneitra. As they crested a hill and descended into a valley, all of a sudden they realized they had walked right into the midst of a minefield. As they tried to figure out what to do in order not to be killed, they determined they would use their knives as they had been trained to locate, dig up, and disarm the mines. However, this would be a slow process, and with dawn coming they would be exposed to the Syrian soldiers. Suddenly out of nowhere a severe wind began to blow with such intensity the soldiers were almost blown off their feet. The windstorm lasted only a few minutes before subsiding. As the wind subsided and they opened their eyes, what they saw shook them to the very core of their being. The wind had blown away the top level of the soil, revealing the location of each and every mine. Had the winds not blown, and had they continued, they would at best be captured and at worst been killed or maimed.

Coincidence? Chance? Luck? Or was it a miracle of God?

The Hand from Heaven Miracle

The Israelis were literally being overrun in the Golan Heights in the first hours of the Yom Kippur War by the Syrian army, who had crossed the eastern border into Israel with 1,400 tanks and men. Israel had been caught off guard. The Israelis deployed their forces of only 200 tanks, only to be largely decimated by the onslaught of the Syrian forces. Avi Dor Kahalani, a veteran of the Six Day War of '67, whose story became a best-selling book entitled *Fury 77*, was the tank company commander. Kahalani was on his radio screaming for reinforcements. He was being told reinforcements were on their way, but they must hold out until they arrived because if the Syrians broke out into the valley there would be no stopping them in their march to Tel Aviv. Kahalani kept radioing as the situation became more dire by the moment, and continued to be told help was on the way. The fact was, help was not coming; there was none to send.

As the battle raged, it came down to just 7 Israeli tanks and a few IDF light helicopters with 2 wire-guided missiles each against over 1,000 Syrian tanks. The Jewish soldiers were certain they were about to meet their maker. Kahalani was firing on the Russian-made T82 tanks and miraculously blowing them away one by one. Suddenly, something happened! The Syrian tanks stopped dead in their tracks. Momentarily, the hatches opened and the tank crews came climbing out and took off running. The Jewish tank crews were in shock. What was happening? They immediately began to advance against their enemy and capture many of the Syrians who held up their arms in surrender.

Later, as the Syrians were being interrogated a recurring story was told. The tank was full of fuel. The gun turret was loaded with a shell and ready to fire. Suddenly it seemed as if a horrendous pressure built up in the cockpit to the point they felt their ears were going to burst. They opened the hatch and as they looked out they saw what seemed to be *a hand from heaven* pressing down upon them. They became horrifically frightened, so they climbed out and ran for their lives.

Granted, this is a pretty wild story and one most would question. However, as the tank crews were being interrogated individually, each one told the exact same story.

Coincidence? Chance? Luck? Or was it God at work?

Let's investigate together and see at what conclusion we arrive.

Gary D. Frazier

Section One:

The Past

Chapter 1

Beginnings and Father Abraham

Now the LORD had said unto Abram, Get thee out of thy country, and from thy kindred, and from thy father's house, unto a land that I will shew thee:

And I will make of thee a great nation, and I will bless thee, and make thy name great; and thou shalt be a blessing:

And I will bless them that bless thee, and curse him that curseth thee: and in thee shall all families of the earth be blessed.

So Abram departed, as the Lord had spoken unto him; and Lot went with him: and Abram was seventy and five years old when he departed out of Haran (Genesis 12:1–4).

In order to understand the miracle of Israel, and by extension the miracles that impact believers — including, of course, *you* — it is critical to read and absorb the early chapters of the Bible, beginning at the beginning, Genesis (the word "Genesis," in Hebrew, means "beginnings").

God had a plan from the very moment of creation, and if we look for His hand in world history, both past and present, we can be certain of His hand in the future.

Let's take a look at history, according to the Bible.

HIStory

It is of the utmost importance that we know *HIStory*. Sadly, many today have no historical reference from which to draw and as such, cannot grasp the present, let alone the future. The majority of people today have been taught history in light of a series of names, places, dates, and seemingly disconnected events. The result of this type of teaching has, for the most part, failed to inspire students to love, appreciate, and respect history as well as see the value of understanding how world events are, in fact, connected one to another.

If one views history through the lens of Scripture, the Bible, and sees God working in the affairs of men and nations with Israel and the Jewish people at the center, then history becomes truly exciting because it validates it is His story!

By the way, many today are unaware that the Bible is the only sacred book in the world that records verifiable history, including the astonishing instances of predictive prophecy.

The question is often asked: Is there really a god who is involved in the affairs of men, or is this a myth, a fairy tale made up by men who are weak and therefore need the concept of a god to worship? Well, we want to share with you how God works in history. People often think the promises of God should be fulfilled instantaneously, and if not, they deny the very existence of the creator.

It doesn't quite work that way.

In Isaiah 46:9–10, we read:

> Remember the former things of old: for I am God, and there is none else; I am God, and there is none like me. Declaring the end from the beginning, and from

ancient times the things that are not yet done. saying,
My counsel shall stand, and I will do all my pleasure.

This is a promise from God. He Himself has already written the
final chapter of history and of each and every life as well. Wow!
Can this be true? Are the steps of my life ordered already? If
this is true, am I only a puppet on the stage of life? Absolutely
not! God, as the Creator, has given each and every one of us the
freedom of choice. We get to choose what we will do. We get to
choose whether or not we will believe and trust God or reject and
deny His existence. This is why God reveals in the above passage
that He already knows and therefore can reveal His plan to the
world. Not because we are puppets on His stage, but because to
Him the future is the past and therefore He has already seen each
and every choice we make. Please remember, time was created
for man. God is timeless, eternal, and therefore He looks *"back
to the future."*

As a result, His promises are always sure. We find no such
claims in other sacred books, such as the Koran, the Hindu
Vedas, or the writings of Buddha or Confucius.

In any event, the Bible tells us clearly how nations — and in
particular, a Nation — came into being.

Despite what you've heard from left-leaning revisionist university professors, liberal preachers, or the media, biblical history
is sound and provable. Although the Bible is not a history book,
50 percent of it is in fact history, and when the Creator records
history, He does so accurately.

The Garden

The first 11 chapters of the Bible set the stage for an unfolding
drama that not only chronicles the creation of all that exists but
gives us a working foundation for the present and a look to the
future. We read those first words, *In the beginning God created.*
Since this is not a book about creation, let us say plainly — yes,
we believe in a Creator and in six literal 24-hour days of creation

as well as a supreme being who spoke the world, and all that is within it, into existence. And no, we do not believe in Frederick Coyle's "big bang" theory no matter how popular the TV show might have become! Then God rested from His work on the seventh day. If you would like to dig into this more deeply, we would refer you to the works of a good friend Ken Ham and his staff at www.answersingenesis.com, as well as Dr. Henry Morris III and the scholars at the Institute for Creation Research at www.icr.org.

These first chapters of Genesis point us to a period of some two thousand years where we find only one kind of people on the earth — Gentiles. As we read, we trace the genealogy and chronology of these created beings whom God intended to leave their fathers and mothers, marry, have families, and care for His creation as they honored Him with holy living and obedience to His commands.

We do not have to read very far until we begin to realize there is a problem. The problem is that the man and woman God had created in His image chose to sin against Him, severing their sweet fellowship with Him. The ensuing years saw the continued rebellion against a holy God and His commands. Sadly, by the time we come to the sixth chapter of Genesis we read these words:

> And God saw that the wickedness of man was great in the earth, and that every imagination of the thoughts of his heart was only evil continually.
>
> And it repented the LORD that he had made man on the earth, and it grieved him at his heart.
>
> And the LORD said, I will destroy man whom I have created from the face of the earth; both man, and beast, and the creeping thing, and the fowls of the air; for it repenteth me that I have made them (Genesis 6:5–7).

As bleak as these words sound, the next verse gives us great hope:

> But Noah found grace in the eyes of the LORD. . . . Noah was a just man and perfect in his generations, and

Noah walked with God. And Noah begat three sons, Shem, Ham, and Japheth (Genesis 6:8–10).

Yes, God did ultimately destroy every living thing on the globe with a worldwide flood. The only exceptions were those whom God brought to safety within the ark built by Noah and his wife, along with their three sons and their wives. Only eight human beings shared the ark, Darren Aronofsky (writer and director of the movie *Noah* [2014] evidently forgot to check the Bible before he made the movie[1] since he added Tubal-Cain with two of every kind of unclean animal, seven of every kind of clean animal, and seven of every kind of bird. (Were there dinosaurs on the ark?[2])

Now here is where it gets interesting. After the Flood, these eight humans emerged from the ark and began the process of re-populating the world. As we read the genealogy of the three sons, this is what we discover. Shem was 98 years old when the Flood ended and the earth became inhabitable once again. Two years later, when he was 100 years old, he began to have sons and daughters and would do so until he died 402 years after the Flood.

As we continue reading the historical narrative, we learn that eventually one of his descendants named Terah would have a son whom he would name *Abram*. Terah dwelt in a

Map showing modern-day Iraq, with Baghdad and the ancient site of Ur noted. (Shutterstock)

---

1. http://www.charismamag.com/blogs/fire-in-my-bones/20140-seven-of-the-worst-mistakes-in-the-movie-noah
2. https://answersingenesis.org.

place called Ur of the Chaldees (Genesis 11:31; today thought to have been in what was Mesopotamia and is today Iraq).

Apparently, Abram was quite a guy because God chose to speak to him and gave him a command associated with a promise.

> Now the LORD had said unto Abram, Get thee out of thy country, and from thy kindred, and from thy father's house, unto a land that I will shew thee: and I will make of thee a great nation, and I will bless thee, and make thy name great; and thou shalt be a blessing: And I will bless them that bless thee, and curse him that curseth thee: and in thee shall all families of the earth be blessed (Genesis 12:1–3).

In this incredible promise, God was setting the stage for a future *miracle* that would ultimately change the world. It was a miracle that would bring a new era upon the earth and that would bring a Savior to fallen humanity. It would be a miracle that would change the course of history forever. The miracle would be known as the *Jews*, and their land would be called *Israel*.

In terms of geographical and family background, Abram's family had settled in a prosperous region. In Genesis 11:31, we read that Terah took his family to a place called Haran (thought to have been somewhere in Mesopotamia). It was there that both Terah and Abram were instructed to leave and go to the land of Canaan.

Now, the land of Canaan, inhabited of course by the Canaanites (descendants of Ham), is still disputed today. Geographically, it is located within the borders of modern Israel. (Incredibly, former Palestinian terrorist leader Yasser Arafat claimed the Palestinians were directly descended from the Canaanites and were therefore

Fascinating Fact

While the Palestinians attempt to claim they are descendants of the Philistines (who came from the Island of Crete), they are in fact from the Saudi peninsula and have been in the land no more than about 200 years.

entitled to the land, rather than the Jews! He should have gotten his story straight since they also claim to be descendants of the Philistines, hence Palestine.)

Terah died in Haran (Genesis 11:32).

> Now the Lord had said unto Abram, Get thee out of thy country, and from thy kindred, and from thy father's house, unto a land that I will shew thee (Genesis 12:1).

It is here that we are introduced to the great promise God made to Abram's descendants:

> And I will bless them that bless thee, and curse him that curseth thee: and in thee shall all families of the earth be blessed (Genesis 12:3).

Notice that the curse is very personal as the Lord uses the pronoun "him." Do you think anti-Jewish tyrants down through history — think Haman (Esther), Hitler, Stalin, and many others — have not been cursed? Abram was obedient, and that made all the difference.

The Covenant

God would take this man Abram, whom He later would rename "Abraham" (Abram = great father, Abraham = father of a multitude), and enter into a covenant with him, which we today must seek to understand fully. This covenant would be without conditions on Abram and his descendants, yet wholly dependent upon the faithfulness of the Creator.

It happened this way: God spoke to Abram and promised him descendants that would be as numerous as the stars in the sky. The problem was that Abram's wife, Sarai, was barren and they had no children. Yet Abram believed what God told him.

> And he said unto him, Take me an heifer of three years old, and a she goat of three years old, and a ram of three years old, and a turtledove, and a young pigeon. And he took unto him all these, and divided them in the

midst, and laid each piece one against another: but the birds divided he not. And when the fowls came down upon the carcases, Abram drove them away.

And when the sun was going down, a deep sleep fell upon Abram; and, lo, an horror of great darkness fell upon him. And he said unto Abram, Know of a surety that thy seed shall be a stranger in a land that is not theirs, and shall serve them; and they shall afflict them four hundred years; And also that nation, whom they shall serve, will I judge: and afterward shall they come out with great substance. And thou shalt go to thy fathers in peace; thou shalt be buried in a good old age. But in the fourth generation they shall come hither again: for the iniquity of the Amorites is not yet full.

And it came to pass, that, when the sun went down, and it was dark, behold a smoking furnace, and a burning lamp that passed between those pieces. In the same day the LORD made a covenant with Abram, saying, Unto thy seed have I given this land, from the river of Egypt unto the great river, the river Euphrates: The Kenites, and the Kenizzites, and the Kadmonites, And the Hittites, and the Perizzites, and the Rephaims, And the Amorites, and the Canaanites, and the Girgashites, and the Jebusites (Genesis 15:9–21).

This covenant, although often ignored and misunderstood, still stands! God, the Creator and owner of the universe and all that is therein, conveys this land to Abraham and his descendants, but only those who would come through the line of his soon-to-be miraculously born son, Isaac.

How much land? It is huge!

. . . from the river of Egypt unto the great river, the river Euphrates: the Kenites, and the Kenizzites, and the Kadmonites, and the Hittites, and the Perizzites, and the Rephaims, and the Amorites, and the Canaanites, and the Girgashites and the Jebusites (Genesis 15:18–21).

Have the Jews ever occupied all the territory God bequeathed them? No. Will they? Yes! When? Check out chapter 8 for the answer, but for now know this, YES! God's covenant is eternal and unconditional.

Have you ever wondered if God has a sense of humor? On many occasions we have. In fact, every time we pause and take a good look at the world in which we live, we become more convinced this is true. For example, what's up with the two-hump camel? How about the platypus?

We could go on and on, but you get the idea. The reason we mention this is because in Genesis 17 God would pay a visit to Abram and Sarai after they had taken matters into their own hands and had a son by Sarai's Egyptian servant girl, Hagar. They named the boy Ishmael, and when he was 12 and Abram was 99, God comes to Abram and has a talk with him. The gist of the conversation is that God tells him He is going to give him another son that Sarai will birth. We can only imagine what Abram thought! *Yeah, right. God, are You kidding me? Just in case You forgot, I'm 99 and Sarai is 89. We're a little old to be having a baby, don't you think?*

It gets better. Abraham fell face down and laughed! Really, that's exactly what he did. He says to himself,

> Shall a child be born unto him that is an hundred years old? and shall Sarah, that is ninety years old, bear? (Genesis 17:17).

So Abraham then offers an alternative and says to God, "O that Ishmael might live before thee!" (Genesis 17:18). In other words, *God we have a son already, and I'm not overly excited about having a baby around, changing diapers and all that!*

God responds and says, "Sarah thy wife shall bear thee a son indeed; and thou shalt call his name Isaac [Isaac means laughter] and I will establish my covenant with him for an everlasting covenant, and with his seed after him" (Genesis 17:19).

Abraham and Sarah's first child, Ishmael, is born through the natural process, but Isaac, the first Jew, is a *miracle of God* and a fulfillment of God's promise to Abraham! God proceeds to tell Abraham that He will bless Ishmael and his descendants and then God adds the big word, BUT! He says,

> But my covenant I will establish with Isaac (Genesis 17:19, 21:11–12).

In one brief but succinct statement, God makes it crystal clear that while He loves the descendants of Ishmael, the covenant concerning the land belongs solely to those who come through the line of Isaac. If we fail to comprehend and accept this truth, we will never understand the issues surrounding this most disputed piece of property that has become the most fought-over piece of real estate in the world.

Fascinating Fact

Muslims reject the Bible because they claim Jews wrote it. In addition, they believe it has been corrupted and therefore the Koran is the only true word from god/Allah.

Israel Is Born

Isaac would have a son and he would name him Jacob, but God would change his name to Israel, which means, *he struggles with God*. The rest of the Old Testament is the historical drama of the Jewish people and their struggling with God in disobedience and the consequences they suffered and continue to suffer even to this day. God's intention was to supernaturally birth a people, an ethnicity that would accomplish at least three purposes:

1. The Jews were to be a *monotheistic* people, in that they would worship the true Creator, as opposed to the pagan peoples who worshiped a plurality of gods.

2. They were to be a *holy* people as opposed to the ungodliness of their neighbors.

3. God intended to showcase the Jews to the world as an example of what He could do for those wholly committed to Him.

They failed miserably on all counts! But God did not, nor would He give up on them.

The Egypt Years

Now, look, one of the early prophecies in the Bible, and one quite remarkable, is given when God tells Abraham:

> And he said unto Abram, Know of a surety that thy seed shall be a stranger in a land that is not theirs, and shall serve them; and they shall afflict them four hundred years; And also that nation, whom they shall serve, will I judge: and afterward shall they come out with great substance (Genesis 15:13–14).

This is incredible; it is one of those moments when God tells humans directly *what will happen*. Don't forget Isaiah 46:9–10. This makes God and the Bible unique in history. Sure enough, that's exactly what happened. You see, Abraham eventually died (at age 175!), and one of his descendants, Jacob, had 12 sons who would become known as the Twelve Tribes of Israel:

Reuben, Simeon, Judah, Issachar, Zebulun, Benjamin, Dan, Naphtali, Gad, Asher, Ephraim, Manasseh.

Fascinating Fact

Although we'll get into this in more detail later, those names will appear on the 12 gates of the New Jerusalem (Revelation 21:12.)

An Amazing Prophecy

A remarkable prophecy appears in Genesis 49. The scene is the gathering of Jacob of his sons, at the time of his death. He tells them that he will reveal what will happen in the last days!

In Genesis 49:10, he makes a somewhat strange statement:

> The sceptre shall not depart from Judah, nor a lawgiver from between his feet, until Shiloh come; and unto him shall the gathering of the people be.

What? What is a scepter, and what is Shiloh? The great scholar Henry Morris explains:

> This important prophecy has been strikingly fulfilled. Although Judah was neither Jacob's firstborn son nor the son who would produce the priestly tribe, he was the son through whom God would fulfill His promises to Israel and to the world. The leadership, according to Jacob, was to go to Judah, but this did not happen for over 600 years. Moses came from Levi, Joshua from Ephraim, Gideon from Manasseh, Samson from Dan, Samuel from Ephraim and Saul from Benjamin. But when David finally became king, Judah held the scepter [a symbolic, ornamental staff] and did not relinquish it until after Shiloh came. "Shiloh" is a name for the Messiah, probably related to the Hebrew word for "peace" (*shalom*) *and meaning in effect, "the one who brings peace."*[3]

Already in Genesis, we see strong references and prophecies looking forward to the Messiah coming, the Messiah being Jesus Christ (there are 14 generations from Abraham to David, and 14 generations from David to the Babylonian captivity, and 14 generations from the captivity to Jesus).

---

3. Henry Morris, *The Defender's Study Bible* (Nashville, TN: Thomas Nelson, 1996), p. 85.

Eventually, one of Jacob's sons, Joseph, would become a high official in Egypt, and because of his position, his father and brothers were able to come to Egypt in order to escape a famine ravaging Canaan. It was those 70 souls who would become a vast nation, one whose very numbers would concern Egyptian officials as the years went by.

Even in this, the Lord was working.

He would send them into bondage in Egypt, and for 400 years they would endure incredible hardships at the hands of their oppressors. However, God had promised Abraham that his descendants would be innumerable and that they would live in the land of Canaan! In God's time, He would raise up a deliverer by the name of Moses.

This man who did not speak well would, by God's power, lead the Jews out of Egypt, through 40 years in the wilderness, and to the shores opposite the Promised Land before his death. The final blow to Pharaoh and the Egyptians would be when God would institute the Passover.

God told Moses that on the 10th day of the month of Nisan the Jewish families were to take a lamb one year of age and take it into their homes where it would become a family pet for four days. On the 14th of that same month, in the evening they were to take the innocent lamb and slit its throat, drain the blood into a basin, take a hyssop branch and make the sign of a cross by wiping the blood on the lintel over the door and the sides of the door, the doorposts. Then, in the night God would send the death angel, and wherever there was a house without the blood applied, the first-born would die (Exodus 12).

It had been 430 years since Jacob and his 11 sons had joined their brother Joseph in Egypt. The first 30 years they had flourished until Joseph died, but then it had been 400 years of living hell under the tyrannical and oppressive rule of the pharaohs. However on this day, the 14th of the Jewish month of Nisan, it all came to an end . . . or had it?

The Wilderness Years

Things in Egypt had been hard, but through the years the descendants of Abraham through Isaac had come to know what to expect from their oppressors more or less, and had managed to survive. This God-given *desire to survive* would become a driving force in the life of the Jewish people in the centuries that lay ahead.

Now they faced the wilderness, the desert, and had little or no experience surviving in this barren, thirsty land. I must pause to remind us at this point that the God who promised is the God who delivers — and deliver He did!

First it was wiping out Pharaoh's entire "cavalry" in the waters of the Red Sea. While the Bible skeptics claim this never happened, evidence was discovered in the Red Sea Gulf of Aqaba in 2003 that substantiates the biblical account and cannot be dismissed. Items discovered were remains of hundreds of bodies, chariot wheels, weapons, and many tools, to name just a few.

An Amazing Prophecy

In one of his last books, *god Is Not Great: How Religion Poisons Everything*, Christopher Hitchens reveals his anti-Bible bias by claiming that the Exodus story never happened. Hitchens was in many ways a brilliant writer, but in this regard he missed badly. His evidence that the Exodus never happened? Merely this:

> It goes without saying that none of the gruesome, disordered events described in Exodus ever took place. It was all [the biblical account], quite simply and very ineptly, made up at a much later date.[4]

---

4. Christopher Hitchens, *god is Not Great* (New York: Hachette Book Group, 2007), p. 102.

Really? Then Mr. Hitchens, and all critics, please explain prophecies such as the one found in Exodus 12:14:

> And this day shall be unto you for a memorial; and ye shall keep it a feast to the LORD throughout your generations; ye shall keep it a feast by an ordinance for ever.

This is quite extraordinary, because in the 3,700 years since this prophecy was given, Jews the world over — many of them not believers — stop what they're doing to observe Passover each year!

Then God delivered their need for water and food. Not just a few drops, but water for approximately two million people. He turned bitter water to sweet water and later would bring water from a rock, manna to sustain them, and finally, quail for meat.

God constantly dazzled the people by miracle after miracle, proving His great love for them as well as His plan of redemption by giving Moses the Ten Commandments. God would further give specific instructions for building the articles to be placed in the temporary Tabernacle.

For 40 years these chosen by God would remain in the wilderness, while God would purge from them those who exhibited unbelief in God's promises concerning the land.

Moses, Joshua, and Caleb would continue to lead and exhort them to simply trust the God who had delivered them. Ponder this thought for a moment: God had entered into

Fascinating Fact

Moses sent 12 spies to spy out the land and 10 came back and reported that while the land was abundant and beautiful there were giants in the land and they could not defeat them! Failure to trust and believe cost these 10 the joy of entering into the Promised Land. Many make the same mistake today. Trust and believe Him!

a covenant and had sworn by Himself with regard to the Jews as His chosen people, and that the Deliverer, the Messiah, would come from or through this lineage. How then could He let them die out? He could not, and He would not!

The Promised Land

After 40 years in the wilderness/desert and the dying off of the unbelieving generation who failed to trust God, the day had finally arrived! The land promised to Abraham's descendants lay just across the rushing waters of the Jordan River. God had brought them out of Egypt and slavery to bring them in to experience freedom from oppression and obedience to God who created, called, and cherished them.

All they had to do now was figure out how in the world they were going to get across this river with two million men, women, and children! But God! He was at work again, just as He had been every step of the way.

God told Moses to appoint Joshua as their leader and for him, that is Moses, to address the people one last time before his departure.

> But the LORD was wroth with me for your sakes, and would not hear me: and the LORD said unto me, Let it suffice thee; speak no more unto me of this matter.
>
> Get thee up into the top of Pisgah, and lift up thine eyes westward, and northward, and southward, and eastward, and behold it with thine eyes: for thou shalt not go over this Jordan.
>
> But charge Joshua, and encourage him, and strengthen him: for he shall go over before this people, and he shall cause them to inherit the land which thou shalt see (Deuteronomy 3:26–28).

Moses then reiterates to the chosen the Ten Commandments and says:

Hear, O Israel: The Lᴏʀᴅ our God is one Lᴏʀᴅ: And thou shalt love the Lᴏʀᴅ thy God with all thine heart, and with all thy soul, and with all thy might (Deuteronomy 6:4–5).

Thus begins the beginning of this overarching story of redemption, promise, and provision. Come with us as we detail the rest of this fascinating story, which culminates on a mountain in Israel, the mountain you can reach despite your own valley experiences in this life!

Chapter 2

The Reign of Judges, Saul, David, and Solomon

M oses was dead and buried! Their leader was gone! But God! God raised up Joshua to lead the Jews to cross the Jordan and enter the Promised Land. The God who had promised to deliver was very much at work. Having crushed Pharaoh, and having protected and provided for them for 40 years, He was not about to let anything happen to His people. First they had to cross a raging river. No problem! God just stopped the water from flowing and they crossed over on dry ground. Remember, they had seen the waters of the Red Sea parted so. . . .

They then marched around the fortified walls of Jericho seven times on the seventh day, and when the trumpet was sounded, they watched as the walls fell. God's hand at work yet again!

This would be the beginning of the conquest of the land God had promised Abraham He would give his descendants through Isaac.

Fascinating Fact
Judges of Israel
1. Othniel
2. Ehud
3. Deborah
4. Gideon
5. Abimelech
6. Tola
7. Jephtah
8. Ibzan
9. Elon
10. Abdon
11. Samson
12. Samuel

But failure to obey God's every command would bring calamity. They began to think rather than obey, and the result was disastrous. In some cases it was outright defeat and death to many. In every case it was God's judgment upon the sin of disobedience. Disobedience would bring judgment, resulting in oppression, resulting in crying out to God for deliverance. This cry would bring a deliverer who God would send to lead them to victory and a time of peace, only to fall back into their previous disobedience and the cycle would start over.

To say the Jews had a short memory would be an understatement for sure. But were they really much different than we are today? We see God at work and yet when the storm comes, we forget that He has delivered us before and He can do it again, and again, and again, if we trust and believe.

Now they wanted a King! Flesh and blood! Someone to talk to and touch!

> And it came to pass, when Samuel was old, that he made his sons judges over Israel.
>
> Now the name of his firstborn was Joel; and the name of his second, Abiah: they were judges in Beersheba. And his sons walked not in his ways, but turned aside after lucre, and took bribes, and perverted judgment. Then all the elders of Israel gathered themselves together, and came to Samuel unto Ramah,
>
> And said unto him, Behold, thou art old, and thy sons walk not in thy ways: now make us a king to judge us like all the nations.
>
> But the thing displeased Samuel, when they said, Give us a king to judge us. And Samuel prayed unto the LORD.
>
> And the LORD said unto Samuel, Hearken unto the voice of the people in all that they say unto thee: for they have not rejected thee, but they have rejected me, that I should not reign over them.

According to all the works which they have done since the day that I brought them up out of Egypt even unto this day, wherewith they have forsaken me, and served other gods, so do they also unto thee.

Now therefore hearken unto their voice: howbeit yet protest solemnly unto them, and shew them the manner of the king that shall reign over them.

And Samuel told all the words of the LORD unto the people that asked of him a king.

And he said, This will be the manner of the king that shall reign over you: He will take your sons, and appoint them for himself, for his chariots, and to be his horse-men; and some shall run before his chariots.

And he will appoint him captains over thousands, and captains over fifties; and will set them to ear (plow) his ground, and to reap his harvest, and to make his instruments of war, and instruments of his chariots.

And he will take your daughters to be confectionar-ies, and to be cooks, and to be bakers.

And he will take your fields, and your vineyards, and your oliveyards, even the best of them, and give them to his servants.

And he will take the tenth of your seed, and of your vineyards, and give to his officers, and to his servants.

And he will take your menservants, and your maid-servants, and your goodliest young men, and your asses, and put them to his work.

He will take the tenth of your sheep: and ye shall be his servants.

And ye shall cry out in that day because of your king which ye shall have chosen you; and the LORD will not hear you in that day.

Nevertheless the people refused to obey the voice of Samuel; and they said, Nay; but we will have a king over us; that we also may be like all the nations; and that our king may judge us, and go out before us, and fight our battles.

And Samuel heard all the words of the people, and he rehearsed them in the ears of the LORD.

And the LORD said to Samuel, Hearken unto their voice, and make them a king. And Samuel said unto the men of Israel, Go ye every man unto his city (1 Samuel 8:1–22).

A model of ancient Jerusalem in the City of David Museum, Jerusalem

And so it was! God was rejected and a man chosen to be king. First would come Saul, followed by David, then Solomon, and then the kings of Israel and Judah. The next approximately 120 years would see God blessing Israel as the scepter passed from Saul to David, a man God said was after His (God's) own heart and finally to Solomon, the wisest man who ever lived. But upon Solomon's death the trouble began, and for the next 300-plus years we read of the steady decline of obedience and worship of the true God. Yes, there were moments of goodness and God's mercy because He was going to bring the Messiah. Moments such as brief returns to God led by Jehoshaphat, Joash, and Hezekiah spurred on by God's prophets, but overall, a sad history being penned in the blood of rebellion.

Chapter 3

The Prophets

> God, who at sundry times and in divers manners spake in time past unto the fathers by the prophets, hath in these last days spoken unto us by his Son, whom he hath appointed heir of all things, by whom also he made the worlds. . . (Hebrews 2–1:1).

> Attacks upon Isaiah, Daniel and other books, because they abound in wonderful predictions, will have weight only with those who deny the fundamentals of Christianity.[1] — Robert Dick Wilson

The first time the word *prophets* appears in the Bible occurs in Numbers 11:29:

> And Moses said unto him, Enviest thou for my sake? would God that all the LORD's people were prophets, and that the LORD would put his spirit upon them!

The word appears 227 times, all through the Old and New Testaments, and refers to someone who proclaims the will of God. Another word is *oracle*. Such a person was a conduit for the Lord to speak to the people.

---

1. Robert Dick Wilson, *A Scientific Investigation of the Old Testament* (Pelham, AL: Solid Ground Christian Books, 2007), p. 143.

Fascinating Fact

Getting *prophecy* and *prophesy* right. *Prophecy* is a noun and is the category dealing with teaching concerning future events. To *prophesy* is a verb and is the proclamation of a specific future event.

In the Bible, the prophets are numerous and God spoke through them to primarily challenge and rebuke the Jews to live in obedience to God. However, God often used the prophets to also foretell how God was going to intervene to protect and deliver His chosen people.

Prophets appeared with many different characteristics, revealing how God can work through multiple personalities. The prophets ranged from Moses to desert "dwellers" like John the Baptist, to palace confidantes (Jeremiah). Apostles such as Peter uttered prophecies, as did more mysterious figures such as Elisha.

Arguably, the first prophecy in the Bible is recorded in Genesis 1:3:

And God said, Let there be light: and there was light.

The Creator said there would be light in the future, and so there was — whether that occurred a few minutes later, or a few hours.

But perhaps the first "hard" prophecy, in the classic sense, comes from Genesis 2:17, in which God warns His human creation not to eat from the Tree of the Knowledge of Good and Evil, located in the garden He had made. In this particular warning/prophecy, God tells Adam that if he eats of the tree, he will "surely die."

This warning leads to a broader prophecy in the next chapter, one that has proven to be pivotal for human history.

In the famous passage from Genesis 3:14–19, God tells both Adam and Eve, and their nemesis, the serpent (Satan), exactly what will happen to them and those who would follow, due to their sin and disobedience:

And the LORD God said unto the serpent, Because thou hast done this, thou art cursed above all cattle, and above every beast of the field; upon thy belly shalt thou go, and dust shalt thou eat all the days of thy life:

And I will put enmity between thee and the woman, and between thy seed and her seed; it shall bruise thy head, and thou shalt bruise his heel.

Unto the woman he said, I will greatly multiply thy sorrow and thy conception; in sorrow thou shalt bring forth children; and thy desire shall be to thy husband, and he shall rule over thee.

And unto Adam he said, Because thou hast hearkened unto the voice of thy wife, and hast eaten of the tree, of which I commanded thee, saying, Thou shalt not eat of it: cursed is the ground for thy sake; in sorrow shalt thou eat of it all the days of thy life; thorns also and thistles shall it bring forth to thee; and thou shalt eat the herb of the field; in the sweat of thy face shalt thou eat bread, till thou return unto the ground; for out of it wast thou taken: for dust thou art, and unto dust shalt thou return.

This passage has been called the "Protoevangelium," the "First Gospel," because in it, God is outlining a coming showdown between His Redeemer, Jesus Christ, and Satan. The reference in Genesis 3:15 is a picture of the ages-long war between Jesus and Satan, who would oppose the Messiah/Redeemer. In the passage, the "seed" of the woman is Jesus, the woman being the Jewish people who were also to come.

This remarkable prophecy sets the stage for all of world history. It is important to note that just as John said in Revelation 19:10:

And I fell at his feet to worship him. And he said unto me, See thou do it not: I am thy fellowservant, and of thy brethren that have the testimony of Jesus: worship God: for the testimony of Jesus is the spirit of prophecy.

Jesus Christ is the redemption story that runs throughout the entire Bible. As we have seen, His coming is prophesied in Genesis 3 and

Genesis 49. The "scarlet thread" of the penalty He paid on the Cross for our sin ties all of Scripture together. Finally triumphant in Revelation, we read in Revelation 22:7 that Jesus will usher in eternity in the New Jerusalem. There, He exhorts believers:

> Behold, I come quickly: blessed is he that keepeth the sayings of the prophecy of this book.

By "quickly," Jesus means that when He returns, it will happen suddenly. In Acts 1:9–11, we read the account of Jesus ascending to heaven after His Resurrection:

> And when he had spoken these things, while they beheld, he was taken up; and a cloud received him out of their sight. And while they looked stedfastly toward heaven as he went up, behold, two men stood by them in white apparel; which also said, Ye men of Galilee, why stand ye gazing up into heaven? this same Jesus, which is taken up from you into heaven, shall so come in like manner as ye have seen him go into heaven.

The location of His ascension is the Mount of Olives, and it is still there, awaiting His return. On the eastern slope of the Mount of Olives is the biblical town of Bethany, and the western slope overlooks the Old City of Jerusalem, directly across from the place where the Jewish temples stood in ancient times.

If you visit Israel, you can stand on the Temple Mount and look across at the Mount of Olives. These real events in history, past, present, and future, hold the great hope of mankind.

In the last week of His life on earth, Jesus talked to the Apostles about many things, including what will happen in the last days. Then, of course, days later He exhorted them to fulfill the Great Commission.

A remarkable prophecy is found in Zechariah 14:1–4:

> Behold, the day of the LORD cometh, and thy spoil shall be divided in the midst of thee. For I will gather all

View to Jerusalem from the olive grove on the Mount of Olives.
(Shutterstock)

nations against Jerusalem to battle; and the city shall be taken, and the houses rifled, and the women ravished; and half of the city shall go forth into captivity, and the residue of the people shall not be cut off from the city.

Then shall the LORD go forth, and fight against those nations, as when he fought in the day of battle.

And his feet shall stand in that day upon the mount of Olives, which is before Jerusalem on the east, and the mount of Olives shall cleave in the midst thereof toward the east and toward the west, and there shall be a very great valley; and half of the mountain shall remove toward the north, and half of it toward the south.

Did you catch that? His feet "shall stand in that day upon the mount of Olives." Few are aware of this prophecy, or the related one found a few chapters earlier:

And I will pour upon the house of David, and upon the inhabitants of Jerusalem, the spirit of grace and of supplications: and they shall look upon me whom they have pierced, and they shall mourn for him, as one mourneth for his only son, and shall be in bitterness for him, as one that is in bitterness for his firstborn (Zechariah 12:10).

The significance of Zechariah 12 is that the Jewish people will finally see their Messiah, and He is Jesus Christ. This is the great acknowledgment in the Old Testament that the God of Abraham, Isaac, and Jacob — the great Creator God — is also Jesus. Remember, in John 10:30, Jesus said, "I and my Father are one."

Chronologically, there is a 400-year "gap" between the Old and New Testaments in the Bible. The last book of the OT is that of the prophet Malachi. It is thought by some conservative scholars that Malachi lived and wrote in the time of Nehemiah.

Malachi's small book is not unimportant, as he boldly looked far into the future, to the time of the "great and dreadful day of the Lord." According to Henry Morris, it is appropriate that Malachi prophesied the coming of John the Baptist, hundreds of years in the future (Malachi 4:5), since the Baptist is considered to be the *first* New Testament prophet!

An Amazing Prophecy

The entire Book of Isaiah is prophetic, and contains some of the most important prophecies of all time, including the establishment of the modern state of Israel.

Yet there is something equally remarkable about the Book of Isaiah that is not well known. It is important, given the fact that many Bible critics claim the Bible itself is not at all divinely inspired. However, do they know. . . .

From Genesis to Revelation, the Bible is comprised of 66 books. The so-called Old Testament (also known as the Hebrew Scriptures) is concerned with God's holiness, His righteousness, and where appropriate, His wrath and judgment. The Old Testament is comprised of 39 books.

The New Testament is comprised of 27 books, focusing on God's grace and mercy.

The Book of Isaiah's first 39 chapters deals with God's wrath and judgment. The final 27 chapters look forward to His grace and mercy in the last days, culminating in the bliss of eternity, where there will be no more suffering.

Wow! Do you get that? Do you understand that the internal evidences that the Bible is divinely inspired destroy the puny arguments of the critics? Just remember the mirror image of the Bible's 66 books alongside the 66 chapters of Isaiah!

The Fabulous Maccabees

In the interim period of the Bible there are still remarkable stories that are the products of previous prophecies. Let's look at some background first.

The Book of Daniel is one of the most discussed and studied prophetic books. Daniel's prophecies have a both "near and far" flavor, meaning some of the prophecies were meant for Daniel's time (the 6th century B.C.), 400 years forward from his time, and the very last days.

It is the 400-year prophecy we want to examine now.

In the time of Daniel, the Jewish people, that is the Southern Kingdom, in their own land, were about to understand the

Fascinating Fact

Both Jewish Temples —
Solomon's and the one
rebuilt in the time of
Herod — were destroyed
by the Babylonians and
Romans, respectively . . .
on the same day, 656
years apart, on the 9th
of Av, according to the
Jewish calendar. This day
is known as Tisha B'Av, a
day of mourning.

consequences of sin. For generations, their leaders had sought to be like the nations around them — and God had warned them against such behavior.

When the cup of the Jewish people was full of sin, God acted by allowing them, the Southern Kingdom of Judah and Benjamin, to be conquered by the Babylonians, based 500 miles east of Jerusalem. In fact, the Babylonian invasion was even more traumatic than that of the Assyrians 200 years prior when the Northern Kingdom was attacked. For it was in Daniel's time that the grand Temple that Solomon had built was destroyed.

While Daniel was concerned about his own time, and that of the very last days of human history — far into the future — he also recorded prophecies that would bring comfort to his people in another dire moment in their collective life.

Daniel's book is intended to show the Jewish people that just as God saved Daniel and his friends from the fiery furnace, He would also save the nation in their greatest moments of peril.

In Daniel, we read prophecies that looked ahead to conquerors like Alexander the Great and Antiochus Epiphanes, who lived in the fourth and second centuries B.C., respectively. In Daniel 11:3–4, we read of the coming Alexander the Great:

> And a mighty king shall stand up, that shall rule with
> great dominion, and do according to his will. And when
> he shall stand up, his kingdom shall be broken, and shall
> be divided toward the four winds of heaven. . . .

Alexander, after racking up amazing conquests, died in 323 B.C. with no heirs, and his kingdom was divided by his four generals, Ptolemy, Selecius, Cassandra, and Lysimachus.

Further in Daniel 11, we read of one who many scholars identify as Antiochus, the fearsome Greek king who waged war through the Middle East; he died in 164 B.C. He is referenced in Daniel 11:31–32 if one accepts the inference:

> **Fascinating Fact**
>
> Antiochus began his assault against the Jews on Sept. 6, 171 B.C., and continued until Dec 25, 165 B.C. when Judas Maccabees restored true worship to the Temple (recorded in the apocryphal book of 1 Maccabees). This matches the 2,300 days of Dan. 8:14.

His armed forces will rise up to desecrate the temple fortress and will abolish the daily sacrifice. Then they will set up the abomination that causes desolation. With flattery he will corrupt those who have violated the covenant, but the people who know their God will firmly resist him (NIV).

That people "who know their God will firmly resist him" were none other than a family of Jews known as the Maccabees. Fearless warriors (think of William Wallace in Braveheart), the Maccabees were determined to throw off the shackles of tyrants like Antiochus and re-establish the kingdom of Israel. So it was that they planned and prosecuted a successful war, and did in fact establish Jewish sovereignty for 100 years, until the Romans exerted control after the time of the Maccabees.

An Amazing Prophecy

Several times in the Bible, as if to "up the ante" as much as possible, God will issue a prophecy heavy with details. One such astonishing prophecy is found in Isaiah 44, the story of Cyrus. Here's the setting, and why it's so amazing.

Isaiah the prophet was recording his prophecies in the 8th century B.C. (think of it like this: more than 700 years before the birth of Christ). He is concerned with, among other things, judgment coming to his people in the form of invading armies. One of those armies in his lifetime, Assyria, wreaked havoc, but nothing like that of the Babylonians 200 years into the future.

Somewhat out of the blue, God Himself declares in chapters 44 and 45 that He would provide an earthly benefactor for the Jewish people . . . but only after they had suffered for 70 years in the Babylonian exile.

Stone projectiles from the Babylonian siege of Jerusalem

Placing Himself clearly infinitely above other "gods" or sacred books, God names the benefactor 150 years before he is born.

Cyrus, the Persian emperor who himself had defeated the Babylonians, would one day allow the Jewish exiles to go back to their land and rebuild. Hear the words of the Lord:

> That saith of Cyrus, He is my shepherd, and shall perform all my pleasure: even saying to Jerusalem, Thou shalt be built; and to the temple, Thy foundation shall be laid (Isaiah 44:28).

More detail is provided in Isaiah 45:1–4 —

> Thus saith the LORD to his anointed, to Cyrus, whose right hand I have holden, to subdue nations before him; and I will loose the loins of kings, to open before him the two leaved gates; and the gates shall not be shut;

I will go before thee, and make the crooked places straight: I will break in pieces the gates of brass, and cut in sunder the bars of iron:

And I will give thee the treasures of darkness, and hidden riches of secret places, that thou mayest know that I, the LORD, which call thee by thy name, am the God of Israel.

For Jacob my servant's sake, and Israel mine elect, I have even called thee by thy name: I have surnamed thee, though thou hast not known me.

Think of it: *God named Cyrus before he was born!* As they usually do, critics claimed that this was recorded after the time of Cyrus, so as to appear to be history instead of prophecy. But there is no evidence for this at all, and it's important to note that the Bible's account is straightforward: chronologically and historically, Cyrus arose long after God named him.

A clay tablet, now known as the Cyrus Cylinder, was discovered in the ruins of Babylon in 1879. Part of the text refers to Cyrus allowing exiles to return to their homeland.

One more proof that God has committed to preserve His people, the Jews, comes from this very story of the Maccabees.

When Antiochus issued decrees that the Jews could not practice their religion, the Jewish priest Mattathias refused to worship the Greek gods. When he died a year later, his son, Judah Maccabee, led a full-scale revolt, using the successful tactic of guerrilla warfare.

In Daniel 11:31–32, we read about the men who would stand up to oppose Antiochus; those men were the Maccabees, and they were destined for their role hundreds of years before they were born.

The Reality of the Prophets

Because Daniel looked ahead and recorded specific details, critical Bible scholars have speculated (and that's all it is) that since man cannot know the future (nor, it seems, the very God the critics claim to know), the "prophecies" must have been merely history written after the fact.

In other words, the critics often like to say that the prophecies were written somewhere around 167 B.C., long after Daniel, as the Jews wanted to create "hero stories" to stir the people to action, and to give them hope.

There is no evidence for any of this, and in fact Bible prophecy stands alone as a foundational proof for the existence of God.

Psalm 122:3 describes Jerusalem as a very compact city; that is certainly true today in the Old City!

Section Two

The Present

Chapter 4

The Jesus Years

For unto us a child is born, unto us a son is given: and the government shall be upon his shoulder: and his name shall be called Wonderful, Counsellor, The mighty God, The everlasting Father, The Prince of Peace.

Of the increase of his government and peace there shall be no end, upon the throne of David, and upon his kingdom, to order it, and to establish it with judgment and with justice from henceforth even for ever. The zeal of the LORD of hosts will perform this (Isaiah 9:6–7).

While the land of Israel had been free for a little over 100 years, the most powerful nation on the map had begun its move into the Middle East, and Israel would fall to the Romans in 63 B.C.

It would be these years that would see the increasing corruption of the religious system in Israel as the office of the high priest would be fought over and in some cases people would be killed in their quest for power and wealth. The Ten Commandments of God were now fragmented into some 613 commands that no one could possibly observe. This religious weight with all its taxes, fear, and servitude was simply too much for the people to bear.

The Pharisees taught there would be a resurrection at the end of time while the Sadducees rejected the notion. The Zealots wanted to overthrow Rome while the Essenes, an extreme sect of the Pharisees, retreated to isolation along the shores of the Dead Sea and sought somewhat of a communal experience preserving the Old Testament manuscripts, baptizing, and believing the end of the world was imminent.

This was the Israel into which the Messiah would be born.

> But when the fulness of the time was come, *God sent forth his Son*, made of a woman, made under the law . . . (Galatians 4:4, emphasis added).

Christ came into the world right on time, Jesus died on time, Jesus was bodily resurrected on time, and Jesus ascended to the Father according to the prophets. "Came on time" in the sense that Daniel had revealed the Messiah would come and be cut off (killed) 483 years from the issuing of a decree to rebuild Jerusalem. While there were many decrees issued by rulers concerning Jerusalem, only one matched the specified criteria of Daniel 9:24–27.

On March 14, 445 B.C., Artaxerxes I issued a decree calling for the rebuilding of Jerusalem and thus began the countdown to the birth, ministry, and death of the Messiah, Jesus of Nazareth.

This amazing prophecy tells us that the Messiah will be killed 483 biblical years from the issuing of the decree. Therefore we can know this event would take place April 10, A.D. 32, and it did!

Fascinating Fact

Did Jesus die on Good Friday? Jews used a lunar calendar of 360 days in a year. Therefore, 483 years times 360 days = 173,880 days. The 173,880 days would run out on A.D. April 6, 32, but on the Jewish calendar it was 10th of Nisan, the very day the Jews were selecting their Passover lamb to be sacrificed on the 14th — Passover! The 10th was Palm Sunday, the 14th was the following Thursday when Jesus was crucified. Find a full explanation at www.garyfrazier.com (free Power Point).

But what about the birth of the Messiah? The Babylonian captivity that began in 605 B.C. and ended in 536 B.C. took place in Babylon, a region of Mesopotamia. The wise men, also known as the Magi, were from this region and were acutely aware of Daniel's prophecy. Therefore, they calculated that if the Messiah were to be killed in April of A.D. 32, He would have to be born sometime around 1 B.C. to A.D. 1. There was yet another clue. According to Jewish law (Numbers 4:3), a rabbi/teacher could not do service in the temple unless he was at least 30 but not yet 50.

> **Fascinating Fact**
>
> Today we are told that Jesus was the first Palestinian. How absurd! Jesus was born in Israel. Israel would not be named Palestine until 135 years later! Jesus was born in Israel, grew up as a Jew in Israel, and died as the King of the Jews in Israel!

Therefore, these wise men took the date of April 32 and deducted 30 years, and given a window of minus a couple of years they began searching the sky for a sign from God, and there it was, a star! A star unlike anything the world had ever seen. This was not a naturally reoccurring phenomenon. It was a miraculous sign from God! They knew it. They followed it. They came to Jerusalem and there inquired as to the place of the birth of the Messiah child. Herod convened the scholars, who stated what Micah the prophet had declared nearly 700 years before.

> But thou, Bethlehem Ephratah, though thou be little among the thousands of Judah, yet out of thee shall he come forth unto me that is to be ruler in Israel; whose goings forth have been from of old, from everlasting (Micah 5:2).

They were not disappointed, as the star moved to a house in Bethlehem, Israel. There they found the baby that was to rule the world. God had come in the flesh and had been born in a stable!

The Lamb of God lay in a feeding trough. Now, nearly two years later, the wise men would worship the King of kings.

Joseph would take Mary and Jesus and flee to Egypt, having received a vision from God, and there they would remain until Herod died. Once the news of Herod's death reached them, they journeyed back to their home of Nazareth where Jesus would grow in stature and in wisdom working alongside His dad, Joseph, under the watchful eye of Mary His mother. Siblings would be born by natural process into the family as the years passed. Journeys to and from Jerusalem during various feast times would occur and Jesus would become familiar with the Jewish laws and customs of the day.

Then the day would come when this young boy of only 12 would dazzle the religious leaders with both His knowledge and His wisdom. Mary watched. Jesus grew. There is hardly an end to the speculation of what Jesus was like in those formative years. Was He seemingly normal, or did He perform some varying types of miracles? Was He so oddly different that people noticed? Did He have normal temptations, etc.? The record is silent. We will never know exactly what type of child/young man He was, but be assured on this one fact: He was God in the flesh from the day He came into the world!

Then everything changed! He turned 30, and as such He was now recognized as a rabbi, a teacher. He turned the water into wine at a wedding in Cana. He called 12 men to follow Him as disciples. He healed the sick. He raised the dead. He fed the hungry. He cast out the demons. He calmed the storms. He exhibited compassion. He spoke with authority. He confounded the religious leaders. He taught His disciples to

> **Fascinating Fact**
>
> Jesus told them at Caesarea Philippi:
> From that time forth began Jesus to shew unto his disciples, how that he must go unto Jerusalem, and suffer many things of the elders and chief priests and scribes, and be killed, and be raised again the third day (Matthew 16:21).

pray, work, and trust Him. He spoke of His impending death, His Resurrection, His going to the Father, and His return. Over and over again He told them, but they just did not understand. How could they? But, the day would come when they would!

It was Passover. Jesus and His team were in Jerusalem. This was the last Passover they would spend together. It was then that Jesus would make an astonishing prophecy concerning what was going to happen to Jerusalem and the Jewish people. The Temple was the setting as the disciples walked with Jesus. He told them the temple and all the beautiful buildings surrounding it would be torn down. He told them not a single stone would be left upon another but all of them cast down! How could this be? The temple was the most fantastic structure in Israel and the first-century world (Matthew 24:1–2).

This shocked them to their core. Later they would ask Him when this would take place. The only way Jesus could know this was going to happen was if He was in fact God. As such, He knew that September 9, A.D. 70, would come. He knew the

Two-thousand-year-old olive trees dot the
Garden of Gethsemane, Jerusalem.

Roman soldiers under Titus would burn the temple. He knew the gold on the walls would melt and run down into the crevices of the stones. He knew the soldiers would use their spears to break apart the rocks. He knew Hadrian, the Roman emperor, would order the ground plowed and a temple to Jupiter built on the site. He knew the command would be given that no Jew may approach this place except to remember the destruction on the 9th of Av. He knew because He is God, and 38 years later it happened! Those still alive remembered.

Further, during that same week on Nisan 10, Palm Sunday, He would prophesy these words:

> And when he was come near, he beheld the city, and wept over it, Saying, If thou hadst known, even thou, at least in this thy day, the things which belong unto thy peace! but now they are hid from thine eyes. For the days shall come upon thee, that thine enemies shall cast a trench about thee, and compass thee round, and keep thee in on every side, And shall lay thee even with the ground, and thy children within thee; and they shall not leave in thee one stone upon another; because thou knewest not the time of thy visitation (Luke 19:41–44).

It happened on the 9th of Av, September 9, A.D. 70.

After a ministry of only 3.5 years, He would die on a Roman cross on the exact day Daniel prophesied. Three days and three nights in a tomb (Matthew 12:40) and then He arose! He would meet with His followers. They would eat together. He

The skull-like rock outcropping at the site of Jesus' crucifixion

would teach them. He would promise them a helper who would come to them. A helper who would guide them into all truth and who would bring to mind all He had taught them.

Forty days would pass and then he was gone. They stood with Him on the Mount of Olives. They watched as He rose into the heavens. Two angels told them He would return again one day to the same place. Then they retreated to a room to wait, to pray — the room where He had washed their feet; the room where He had prayed for them; the room where they had eaten, sung a psalm, and then gone out. It would be the same room where ten days later the promised Holy Spirit would come. They would never be the same! Filled with His presence. Anointed with His power! Overcome with His Joy! They preached! They healed! They served! They were relentlessly persecuted. They suffered! The Church exploded! They were martyred one by one! But they knew! He's alive!

Yes, the destruction of Jerusalem would take place as Jesus said. The Jews would be sold into the slave markets of the world. Simon Bar Kochba would lead a second unsuccessful revolt against Rome in the years 132–35. Estimates are that between 500,000 and 1,000,000 were slaughtered. Hadrian, the Roman emperor, would change the name of Jerusalem to Aelia Capitolina. Israel would become Syria Palestinia, hence the name Palestine. Some 1878 years would pass and the world would largely forget about Israel, and the Jewish homeland would languish under foreign power after foreign power, ruler after ruler who cared nothing for the land let alone the chosen people of God. The Romans, Byzantines, Persians, Arabs, Muslims, Seljuks, Crusaders, Mamelukes, Ottoman Turks, and finally the British. They would all rule this land God had promised to Abraham's descendants through Isaac. But not forever! God's hand was at work in history.

Chapter 5

Next Year in Jerusalem

That then the LORD thy God will turn thy captivity, and have compassion upon thee, and will return and gather thee from all the nations, whither the LORD thy God hath scattered thee.

If any of thine be driven out unto the outmost parts of heaven, from thence will the LORD thy God gather thee, and from thence will he fetch thee: And the LORD thy God will bring thee into the land which thy fathers possessed, and thou shalt possess it; and he will do thee good, and multiply thee above thy fathers (Deuteronomy 30:3–5).

Although there has always been a Jewish presence in their ancestral land — going back to Abram — the final exile initiated by the Romans in the first and second centuries caused the Jewish people to be scattered all over the world, just as the prophets predicted.

For more than 1,878 years, the Jews called virtually every nation on earth home. Because it was "taking so long," even people who were aware of the biblical prophecies became skeptical. Reports are that rabbis in Europe circa late 19th and early 20th century actually met on occasions to consider removing the prayer *Next Year in Jerusalem* from their prayer book. They reasoned it had been so long and they now had new and deep roots in the countries where they resided. Why leave their homes, their livelihoods, and their neighbors, and go to a barren place?

But the Sabbath prayer *Next Year in Jerusalem,* a famous theme in the Bible and in history, is planned and executed solely by the Lord Himself. In Scripture, we are told why:

> Therefore say unto the house of Israel, thus saith the Lord GOD; I do not this for your sakes, O house of Israel, but for mine holy name's sake, which ye have profaned among the heathen, whither ye went (Ezekiel 36:22).

That is, partly because He is aware how the nations view Him and His Chosen People, God must redeem them both physically (a return to the land) and spiritually (a return to the Lord). This He will do, and in fact, is doing.

Gentiles, especially Christians, have little understanding of the Jewish people and in particular, many resent the "choseness" label, not realizing it is not something the Jews asked for, and in fact they have suffered greatly because of.

Further, a little-known fact is that especially in Europe in the Middle Ages, the Jews were not allowed by law to hold specific jobs. Medieval anti-Semitism was a huge problem, and because of the marginalization of Jewish people in their communities, they were forced to become moneylenders. This form of usury itself has become an anti-Semitic label, as Jews were forced to use their intelligence and skills to become financiers.

So it was that Jewish communities were always vulnerable to anti-Jewish fervor. In places like Russia, the so-called "pogroms" (anti-Jewish violence) either resulted in the murder of scores of Jews, or their migration to safer environments.

Because relatively few people in our world have actually read the Bible (including many evangelicals!), few are aware of the huge priority God gives the return of the Jewish people to the land in the last days.

Because God ordained it in order to fulfill His promises to mankind at the end of history, it is vital that the Jewish people are back in their ancestral land. In fact end-times prophecy cannot be fulfilled without the Jews back in their land! Again, for the longest time, this was considered to be a fantasy, even as late as World War II!

Our friend, the Israeli political cartoonist Yaacov Kirschen, once recounted how he grew up listening to dinner table conversations about a whole host of issues including the return to Jerusalem.

In the 30's and 40's, this was part of the conversation. At that time, only a few rabbis and a few crazy American preachers actually believed the Jews would return to Palestine. But then . . . it happened![1]

Fascinating Fact

The land of Israel was renamed *Syria Palestina* by Hadrian, the Roman Emperor, following a second revolt against Rome in A.D. 132–135. The Philistines had always been the enemy of the Jews and as such it was an insult to the Jewish people.

Indeed it did.

The birth of the state of Israel is, to be sure, a key moment. But we have to realize that the substantial ingathering of Jews to Palestine has been going on in earnest since the 1880s. The Russian pogroms were a key driver for this migration to the arid, bleak landscape of Palestine.

Samuel Clemens, better known as Mark Twain, visited the Holy Land in 1867 with a band of some 40 pilgrims. He would later write about his experiences in his 1869 classic titled, *The Innocents Abroad*. Twain wrote:

Of all the lands there are for dismal scenery, I think Palestine must be the prince. The hills are barren, they are dull of color, they are unpicturesque in shape. The valleys are unsightly deserts fringed with a feeble vegetation

---

1. Conversation with the authors.

Samuel Clemens (Mark Twain) from Abdullah frères via Wikimedia Commons

that has an expression about it of being sorrowful and despondent. The Dead Sea and the Sea of Galilee sleep in the midst of a vast stretch of hill and plain wherein the eye rests upon no pleasant tint, no striking object, no soft picture dreaming in a purple haze or mottled with the shadows of the clouds. Every outline is harsh, every feature is distinct, there is no perspective — distance works no enchantment here. It is a hopeless, dreary, heartbroken land.

Palestine sits in sackcloth and ashes. . . . Nazareth is forlorn. . . . Jericho the accursed lies in a moldering ruin. . . . Bethlehem and Bethany, in their poverty and humiliation, have nothing about them now to remind one that they knew the high honor of the Saviour's presence. Renowned Jerusalem itself, the stateliest name in history, has lost all its ancient grandeur and is become a pauper village; the riches of Solomon are no longer there to compel the admiration of visiting Oriental queens; the wonderful temple, which was the pride and glory of Israel is gone, and the Ottoman crescent is lifted above the spot where, on that most memorable day in the annals of the world, they reared the Holy Cross. The noted Sea of Galilee, where Roman fleets once rode at anchor and the disciples of the Saviour sailed in their ships, was long ago deserted by the devotees of war and commerce, and its borders are a silent wilderness; Capernaum is a shapeless ruin; Magdala is the home of beggared Arabs, Bethsaida and Chorazin have vanished from the earth, and the "desert places" round about them, where thousands of men once listened to the Saviour's voice and ate the miraculous bread, sleep in the hush of a solitude that is inhabited only by birds of prey and skulking foxes.

Palestine is desolate and unlovely. . . . Palestine is no more of this workday world. It is sacred to poetry and tradition — it is dreamland.[2]

Describing the Jezreel Valley he opined, "There is not a solitary village throughout its whole extent — not for thirty miles in either direction." Twain's description is perhaps one of the best available to help us understand the deplorable condition of this once beautiful and sacred place. Those who came and went cared nothing for the land — cutting down the forest, polluting the waters of the Jordan as well as the Sea of Galilee, and generally neglecting erosion and its devastating effects.

But God had not forgotten His promise! The Jews would do what no other people had ever done. They would return to a land they had been separated from for almost 1,900 years and begin again by His grace, mercy, and faithfulness.

The year was 1878. The place was a barn outside Paris, France. The man was a Russian-born Jew, Eliezer Ben Yehouda. He believed God had given him a vision as he slept. The vision concerned a command to reintroduce the Hebrew language in Palestine. At the time of the vision, Jews were scattered all over the world, speaking just about every language except Hebrew! Hebrew was a language reserved only for prayers and largely unknown to the Jewish people. The crowds of thousands gathered at the Wailing Wall in Jerusalem for Sabbath prayers were shocked when they heard Yehouda speaking in this language, this dialect. In fact they were so stunned by what they felt was blasphemy they almost stoned him. But he stood firm, believing God had told him to do this. It is difficult to have a relationship with people when they do

2. Mark Twain, *The Innocents Abroad* (New York: Penguin Group, 1966). The Signet Classics text is reprinted from the first printing, which was published in 1869 by the American Publishing Company, Hartford, CT.

not speak the same language. God was going to reverse what He had done at the Tower of Babel! He and He alone could resurrect a language that had not been spoken for centuries and that is what He did in preparation for His chosen to return!

Return to Zion

A definition here is in order: Zion refers to Jerusalem itself, and is first found in Scripture in 2 Samuel 5:7:

> Nevertheless David took the strong hold of Zion: the same is the city of David.

Throughout Scripture "Zion" can refer to Jerusalem, Israel as a whole, or the Temple Mount. Whatever the context, Zion is a thoroughly Jewish concept.

The great British scholar (and Churchill biographer) Sir Martin Gilbert, in his masterful work, *Israel*, provides us with a glimpse into the very "genesis" of the return:

> By the middle of the nineteenth century about 10,000 Jews lived in Palestine. More than 8,000 of them lived in Jerusalem. A few hundred lived in the holy city of Safed, in the north, where several Jewish sages were buried, in the mountain village of Peki'in (which had a tradition of continuous Jewish settlement since Roman times) and in nearby Tiberias on the Sea of Galilee.
>
> In the coastal town of Acre lived 140 Jews, mostly pedlars and artisans, but many without any means of support. There were several hundred Jews in Jaffa. Most of the Jews in Palestine were immigrants from Poland and Lithuania. Many of them survived on charity, sending regular begging letters back to their original communities in Europe, and even dispatching special emissaries to raise funds. But the attraction of Palestine was growing.[3]

---

3. Martin Gilbert, *Israel: A History* (New York: RosettaBooks), kindle edition, 6/5/2014, p. 3–4.

Gilbert also outlines the sketch that became Jewish communities in the Holy Land:

> In 1878 a number of Jews from Jerusalem decided to establish a Jewish village in the Palestinian countryside. Their first effort was to buy some land near Jericho, but the Sultan refused to allow ownership to be transferred to Jews. They did manage to buy land from a Greek landowner in the coastal plain, and named their village Petah Tikvah (Gateway of Hope), but malaria, disappointing harvests, and quarrels among them led to failure. By 1882, when they abandoned the village, there were only ten houses and sixty-six inhabitants. Also founded in 1878, by religious Jews from Safed who wanted to earn their own livelihood, and not be dependent on charity, was the village of Rosh Pina.
>
> Lacking funds and experience, and frequently harassed by the Arabs from nearby villages, they gave up after two years, but Romanian Jews, driven from Romania by persecution and poverty, renewed the settlement in 1882, and obtained sufficient aid from the French Jewish philanthropist Baron Edmond de Rothschild to survive. Growing tobacco and planting mulberry trees for silkworms were two of their enterprises.

Jews draining swamps and reclaiming the land of Israel, 1894

Like so many of the Jewish settlements that were to be found in Palestine, the name of Rosh Pina was taken from a biblical phrase, in this case the "head stone" from Psalm 118: "The stone which the builders refused is become the head stone of the corner. This is the Lord's doing. It has become marvelous in our eyes." In Russia, following an upsurge of violent attacks against Jews — the pogroms — two movements were founded urging the emigration of Jews to Palestine to work as farmers on the Land of Israel (Eretz Yisrael) in order to "redeem" it.[4]

From these very modest beginnings came the national movement known as "Zionism." The word refers simply to the right of the Jews to settle their ancestral homeland, the word "Zion," as we've said, referring to God's work through the Jewish people.

Theodor Herzl's modern, political dream to find a sanctuary for the Jewish people was bound up in biblical history. For those paying attention — and there were not many — the migration of Jews to Palestine was on the horizon in the 19th century.

The British Mandate and the Balfour Declaration gave Jews the world over a tremendous boost, and they anticipated that statehood might happen any day! But as we have seen and will see, the Lord's timetable in the lives of both individuals and nations is often quite different.

Geopolitical forces were at work after 1917, and the momentum from the Balfour Declaration dissipated. Pro-Jewish British lawmakers were slowly replaced by the so-called "Arabists." Remember, at this time in the Middle East, an almost priceless commodity had just been discovered: black gold. Oil!

Increasingly in Europe and America, oil production became an all-consuming pursuit. The discovery of huge oilfields in what had long been known as Mesopotamia, along with the formation of new countries after the 1st World War, pushed the idea of Jewish statehood into the background.

4. Ibid., p. 5.

Arab Muslims have always hated the Jews, and that feeling didn't wane in the 19th and 20th centuries.

Sadly, even American officials were infected with anti-Semitism, none more than President Woodrow Wilson's Secretary of State, Robert Lansing. Israeli scholar and former Israeli ambassador to the U.S. Michael Oren describes the following attempts to bar Jews from settling Palestine.

Lansing warned, "Many Christian sects and individuals would undoubtedly resent turning the Holy Land over to the absolute control of the race credited with the death of Christ." Lansing's reservations about Zionism were shared by other American diplomats. Samuel Edelman, head of the State Department's Near East Intelligence Unit and himself a Jew of German extraction, depicted Zionism as the product of pedestrian eastern European Jews who would have a "polluting and intolerable" effect on Palestine. America's ambassador to Britain, Walter Hines Page, considered Zionism "sentimental, religious . . . unnatural and fantastic" and recommended that the United States give it no further consideration.[5]

Oren recounts the first moments in which Westerners began to cozy up to Arab sheiks and tribal leaders. The Saudis first allowed Americans to launch a survey of Arabian geography in 1929, and in 1932 a quiet engineer from Vermont, Karl S. Twitchell, set out:

> To prove his hunch, Twitchell set out from the Red Sea port of Jidda in February 1932 and trudged over four hundred miles inland. On the outskirts of Medina, he succeeded in identifying an ancient gold mine, which he then reactivated and restored to profitable production. But the proceeds from the mine could not compensate the Saudis for the loss of pilgrimage

---

5. Michael B. Oren, *Power, Faith, and Fantasy: America in the Middle East: 1776 to the Present* (New York: W.W. Norton & Company), kindle edition, 2/17/2008, p. 364.

revenue and the kingdom still faced insolvency. Twitchell continued his search, journeying an additional six
hundred miles to the Persian Gulf, without finding a
single resource of worth, not even water. The situation
appeared irremediable when, on June 1 of that year,
engineers from the Standard Oil Company of California (SOCOL) suddenly struck oil on the barren Gulf
island of Bahrain.[6]

This discovery helped solidify the relationship between Americans, the British, and Arab sheiks. That didn't bode well for
Jewish statehood.

Even the great Winston Churchill sent mixed signals regarding the Jews and Palestine. On the one hand:

> He worked diligently but ultimately unsuccessfully
> to fashion a postwar Middle Eastern settlement that
> included a Jewish state. He also pushed for closer relations
> with the State of Israel from shortly after its founding in
> 1948 through his second premiership in the 1950s. Yet, he
> avoided contemplating or raising Jewish claims to Pales-
> tine when the government — in which he held the senior
> post of first Lord of the Admiralty — deliberated a post-
> war Middle East in 1915, neither said nor wrote anything
> about the Balfour Declaration when it was issued in 1917
> by a government in which he was a mid-level minister of
> munitions, disparaged the Zionist movement in the late
> 1910s and early 1920s, committed 75 percent of Palestine
> to an Arabian prince in 1921 as colonial secretary with-
> out even consulting the Zionists, did little to help Jewish
> settlement in Palestine in the economically depressed late
> 1920s when he was chancellor of the exchequer, and virtu-
> ally abandoned the Zionists following the Second World
> War as head of the political Opposition when they battled

---

6. Ibid., p. 413.

British troops and invading Arab armies in their arduous quest for an independent state.[7]

However . . . remember that the Lord doesn't need men, He merely uses them to fulfill His purposes. Men like Churchill did just enough to propel forward the return.

An Amazing Prophecy

Moses Montefiore and Zechariah 2

I lifted up mine eyes again, and looked, and behold a man with a measuring line in his hand.

Then said I, Whither goest thou? And he said unto me, To measure Jerusalem, to see what is the breadth thereof, and what is the length thereof.

And, behold, the angel that talked with me went forth, and another angel went out to meet him, and said unto him, Run, speak to this young man, saying, Jerusalem shall be inhabited as towns without walls for the multitude of men and cattle therein (Zechariah 2:1–4).

One of the most amazing (though largely unknown) prophecies from the Old Testament found its fulfillment around the time of the American Civil War.

For centuries after the Jews' dispersion from the land, Jerusalem had become a backwater town, far different from its ancient reputation as a famous city. Its buildings were old and crumbling, the walls had been repaired numerous times, and the dwellings inside the walls were densely packed together (as the Psalmist had recorded in Psalm 122:3). The problem was that overcrowding and

---

7. Michael Makovsky, *Churchill's Promised Land: Zionism and Statecraft* (New Haven, CT: Yale University Press), kindle locations 85–86.

the absence of sewer and drainage systems contributed to illness and disease. It wasn't a fun place to live. Help, though, was on the way in the form of a wealthy Jewish benefactor from London.

But let's back up just a minute.

Among the last days' prophecies recorded by Zechariah (a Hebrew prophet who lived about 500 years before Christ) is a curious note early on in the book that bears his name. It seems that just before the return of the Lord in the last days, Jerusalem was to spread out from inside the cramped ancient walls, to include areas outside the walls.

In ancient times, this would have been unthinkable, since ancient cities were encircled by high, stone walls to keep out wild animals, bandits, and rival nations. Safety was paramount.

When Zechariah recorded his prophecies, no one in his right mind would live outside the city walls, especially at night. So what was God telling us in Zechariah 2:4?

Well, first, He was providing us a prophecy so detailed its fulfillment shouldn't be missed. Second, it signaled, as do thousands of other prophecies, that God alone is in control and brings history to the conclusions He has ordained (Isaiah 46:9–10).

Jerusalem emerges in biblical history as "Salem," which is referred to in Genesis 14. By the time of Abraham, it was one of the key cities of the Canaanite civilization.

Later, David bought the threshing floor (2 Samuel 24:24) from Araunah the Jebusite. Jews believe that the site of today's Temple Mount in Jerusalem is biblical Mt. Moriah, where Abraham was prepared to sacrifice Isaac.

In any event, for all its existence, Jerusalem had been a walled city. Beginning in the second century A.D., Jerusalem fell into ruin and remained so until the conscience of one Moses Montefiore was pricked by the plight of the

Jews (and others) who suffered from malnutrition and disease in the crowded city.

So . . . it is doubtful that Montefiore was moved by ancient biblical prophecies. However, he did put his money where his mouth was in improving living conditions for Jerusalemites, beginning in 1860.

The London financier and philanthropist (born to Italian Jews) provided the funds to begin building dwellings outside Jerusalem's city walls.

Naturally, the city's rag-tag residents hesitated to move out into what was still a danger zone (American author Mark Twain would visit the region in 1867, and traveled with bodyguards as they rode on horseback through the parched countryside).

Finally, though, enough people tried it that the first "subdivision" outside the city walls became known as Mishkenot Sha'ananim ("Peaceful Habitation"). There, a

The fulfillment of Zechariah 2:4; today, "Mishkenot Sha'ananim" (Peaceful Habitation) is an artist's colony overlooking Jerusalem's Old City.

series of apartment-like dwellings fronted small, individual vegetable gardens.

Slowly ... slowly ... the community took root, so that its residents could finally enjoy open-air living which, combined with the ability to grow food, drastically improved the lives of the residents of Jerusalem.

Today, Mishkenot Sha'ananim is an upscale artists' colony, and is host to various cultural presentations. Its original apartments have been remodeled to become luxurious accommodations for writers and artists, and the community is easily seen from the Old City's Jaffa Gate. A large windmill that served the original community is the most prominent landmark.

Truly, Zechariah 2:4 has been fulfilled to the letter! Today, visitors can walk down from King David Street, through Mishkenot Sha'ananim and the adjoining Yemen Moshe neighborhood and enter into the Old City. It is an astonishing fulfillment of prophecy, and one that we can see with our own eyes.

But let's not forget the opening part of Zechariah 2. It is also part of the fulfillment. A habitation outside the city walls was important for the fulfillment of Zechariah's prophecy, but a parallel plan for the residents who would stay inside the walls was also important. Thus was a plan conceived to "measure" the city so that modern plumbing could be installed! From an 1864 report by a British surveyor, Captain Wilson:

The Ordnance Survey of Jerusalem

Early in the year 1864 the sanitary state of Jerusalem attracted considerable attention; that city, which the Psalmist had described as "beautiful for situation, the joy of the whole earth," had become one of the most unhealthy places in the world, and the chief reasons assigned for this melancholy change were, the inferior quality of the water and the presence of an enormous mass of rubbish which had been accumulating for centuries. With the rubbish it was hardly possible to deal, but the water supply seemed an easier matter, and several schemes were proposed for improving it, either by repairing the ancient system, or by making new pools, cisterns, and aqueducts. Before, however, any scheme could be carried out, it was necessary to obtain an accurate plan of the city, and with this view Miss Burdett Coutts, a lady ever ready to promote good works, placed a sum of 500 pounds in the hands of a committee of gentlemen interested in Jerusalem.[8]

And there you have it, the first survey done of the Old City of Jerusalem. Combined with the establishment of Mishkenot Sha'ananim, the whole of Zechariah 2:1–4 took final shape in the late 19th century.

Today, we marvel at yet another example of God's hand in history and the fulfillment of Bible prophecy, this one specifically spotlighting a little-known piece of Jewish history!

8. The Palestine Exploration Society, No. 1. First Statement, July 1871. New York: The Palestine Exploration Society Committee, p. 7 and 8; https:// books.google.com/books?id=db04AQAAMAAJ&printsec=frontcover&- source=gbs_ge_summary_r&cad=0#v=onepage&q&f=false).

Chapter 6

The State of Israel Is Born

> Who hath heard such a thing? who hath seen such things? Shall the earth be made to bring forth in one day? or shall a nation be born at once? for as soon as Zion travailed, she brought forth her children (Isaiah 66:8).

These seminal words conveyed by the prophet became a reality! God was at work keeping His promise.

> Behold, I will gather them out of all countries, whither I have driven them in mine anger, and in my fury, and in great wrath; and I will bring them again unto this place, and I will cause them to dwell safely (Jeremiah 32:37).

Anyone with Jewish friends has heard the simple, poignant question, probably many times: "Why?"

For 4,000 years, the Jewish people have been hated by too many. Even today, Israel is not allowed to sit on the Security Council at the U.N. This despite the presence of nations like Saudi Arabia sitting on the Security Council!

For too long, the United Nations has lambasted Israel at every opportunity. In 1975, the infamous "Zionism = Racism" resolution showed clearly that not only are Israel's enemies numerous; they are also immoral.

But it was the lead-up to the creation of this international body that imprinted on the Jewish experience.

The Holocaust

Too few Christians have any real idea what the Holocaust was. They don't understand that the Jews have been harassed for centuries with the "Christ killers" blood libel. The Catholic Church (and now even some evangelicals) accused the Jewish people of collective guilt in the death of Christ, even though the Messiah Himself said that *no one took His life, but that He laid it down willingly* (John 10:18). Further, the Word of God makes it clear. *"For all have sinned and come short of the glory of God"* (Romans 3:23) and as such contributed to Christ's sacrificial death, through our sin problem.

The truth is, the Church overall has linked arms with Israel's enemies ideologically. For example, the PLO's fiendish leader, Yasser Arafat, fanned the flames often by accusing the Jews of killing Christ.

Nary a peep from Western leaders, political or religious. Indeed, Arafat spent 13 nights in the Lincoln Bedroom at the White House, and all the while then President Bill Clinton ignored Arafat's lies regarding the Jewish people.

Anti-Semitism, though, has plagued humanity from the beginning (remember the Genesis 3:15 reference?). In recent times, it reached the boiling point in Europe and the result was six million dead Jews. Hitler almost succeeded in making Europe "judenrein" (Jew free).

In the years before the rise of the Nazis, the so-called "German Christian Movement" did an odd thing: they ignored or spiritualized the Old Testament during church services. Liturgies were altered to minimize Jewish history in the Bible.

The obvious historical truth is, the Bible is thoroughly Jewish: writers, places, and philosophy.

The end result of sanitizing Jewish history in the churches, along with the late-life anti-Semitic views of Martin Luther (he followed the lead of the early Church fathers on this issue) was the murder of Europe's Jews, who were gassed and their bodies burned in the ovens at extermination camps in Germany and Poland.

What explains this type of hatred? What explains the horror of Nazi soldiers smashing Jewish babies against stone walls? What is the reason for the cold, compassionless separation of families at Auschwitz, Dachau, Buchenwald, Ravensbruck, and others?

Just one of almost countless accounts comes from Hana Greenfield's memoir, *Fragments of Memory*. In it, she tells of the Jews' experience with "Christians," as Jewish prisoners were forced to work cleaning up Allied bombing damage:

> We work all day under the supervision of SS men and SS women dressed in their green uniforms. They come in pairs. They sit around guarding us; they talk and laugh, eat and drink, and when they become bored, they hit us.[1]

It got worse.

> It is beginning to get dark when we return to camp through Hamburg's suburbs. Through the windows of the houses we can see decorated Christmas trees in every living room. It all looks so inviting, so warm and so beautiful. It all seems so abnormal in our dreary prisoners' life. Walking wearily in the snow, dragging one tired foot after the other, I become lost in my thoughts: "It would be nice to be a Christian just for one evening. To warm up my frozen feet in that cozy lit living room, to fill my hungry, shrunken stomach with some warm food and maybe fall asleep in a real bed?" "Marsch, marsch! Schnell, schnell!" the SS women guards start screaming

---

1. Hana Greenfield, *Fragments of Memory: From Kolin to Jerusalem* (Jerusalem; New York: Gefen Publishing House), kindle locations 480–484, 10/30/2006.

at us, for they also want to get back to the camp. It is Christmas Eve! Hungry, dirty and exhausted, we reach the gate of the camp in the dark. After another roll call and a body search, a ration of bread and a bowl of watery soup are received by whoever has the strength to stand in line for it. Another day ends. HEILIGE NACHT . . . STILLE NACHT . . . HOLY NIGHT . . . SILENT NIGHT. . . .[2]

This is the experience many Jews have had with Christianity. Christians seem to be unaware of this, for it was essentially, officially Christians who murdered Europe's Jews.

One cannot explain this special level of hatred apart from the Bible.

Reinhard Heydrich, born into a Prussian Catholic family, was 37 years old when he led a high-level meeting at the Wannsee Conference in early 1942. The purpose of the meeting was to devise effective methods of murdering the Jews of Europe.

Hitler called Heydrich "the man with the iron heart."

Think of it: even as the Nazis were losing the war, in the war's final months, they earmarked precious weapons and manpower for the continued killing of Jews! It seems clear to us that this kind of hatred is satanically inspired.

A railroad car that transported Jews to their deaths during the Holocaust; Yad Vashem, Jerusalem

2. Ibid.

When American and British troops liberated the death camps in the spring of 1945, they were shocked at the sheer scope of the Nazi killing machine.

What began in the 1930s, with the herding of Jewish families onto cattle cars, to be transported to the extermination camps, ended with a relatively few Jews huddling and shivering in the sunlight of the war's end.

And yet . . .

From the literal ashes of the Holocaust, God still had a plan for the Jewish people. Although it is difficult for the Jewish people to even understand why the Holocaust happened, it is perhaps even more difficult for them to grasp the fact that Israel and the Jewish people are eternal. God had not abandoned them nor would He. He was still at work as His plan moved on. Did God send these horrible events? Is God the author of evil? The answer is a thousand times NO! God loves His creation. However, the wickedness and evil that lurk in the fleshly heart of man should never be underestimated nor should one discount the demonic activity among mankind. But God did *use* the evil to ultimately drive the Jews back to their land!

One of the loveliest verses in all the Bible is found in Jeremiah 31:3 —

> The LORD hath appeared of old unto me, saying, Yea, I have loved thee with an everlasting love: therefore with lovingkindness have I drawn thee.

While there are plentiful examples in Scripture of the punishments fated to the Jews, there are as many promises of a wonderful future. Hear the Word of the Lord:

> Thus saith the LORD of hosts; In those days it shall come to pass, that ten men shall take hold out of all languages of the nations, even shall take hold of the skirt of him that is a Jew, saying, We will go with you: for we have heard that God is with you (Zechariah 8:23).

When the Lord returns to establish His righteousness, people will actually seek out Jews and ask to go up to Jerusalem with them, in order to worship the Lord together.

What a wonderful promise!

The Holocaust was such a stain on human history that many forget the miracle that came from it. At the very moment the Nazis were working furiously to "finish the job," the organization that came to be known as the Israel Defense Forces was forming in Palestine.

This is an astonishing miracle, that an ancient people would be preserved in their exile, returned to their ancestral land, and would then flourish in that land.

The stage in 1945 was thus set for a clear sign that God is alive and works in the affairs of men today.

An Amazing Prophecy

The only book in the Bible that doesn't mention God explicitly is the Book of Esther.

The book concerns the Jewish holiday of Purim, commemorating the deliverance of the Jewish people from the plot of the evil Haman. In this story, Haman was a high official in the Persian Empire, and he hated the Jews of the kingdom. Through the machinations of Haman, a gallows was built, on which the Jews would be executed. Read the story for yourself, but through the influence of Queen Esther, her people were saved and, in fact, Haman and ultimately his ten sons were hanged on those very gallows!

Not only is the Purim story told in the Book of Esther, but there is a "hidden" prophecy that looks far into the future . . . to the time of the Nazis, another barbaric group determined to eliminate the Jews.

In Esther 9:6–10, we read of Haman's ten sons, who were hanged on the gallows intended for the Jews. It seems that three letters in that series of names — Taf, Shin, and Zayin — are written smaller than the rest, and that this represents a prophecy, as the letters correspond to the Hebrew year 5707 (or 1946).

In October 1946, ten Nazi war criminals were hanged at Nuremberg. As the notorious Julius Streicher was led to the gallows, he blurted out, "Purim, 1946!" It was as if he almost involuntarily screamed the fulfillment of the prophecy that he somehow understood.

A prophecy, or weird coincidence? We believe it is clearly the fulfillment of a strange and electrifying prophecy. The Lord's anger at the enemies of His people burns hot, and His justice has both near and far fulfillment.

Reborn!

Precisely at 4 p.m. on May 14, 1948, the nation of Israel was born. In the very room the authors have stood in many times, Prime Minister David Ben-Gurion read the declaration. (The

The Palestine Post, May 15, 1948

actual document was written in Hebrew!) And in so doing, the world saw the literal fulfillment of the promise that God made by the prophets, to gather the Jewish people up and put them in their land.

It was a monumental moment because it began the *"Terminal Generation,"* the beginning of the last days. Israel must exist in its land for the prophecies to be fulfilled.

The chosen people of God have now returned to their traditional homeland after having been scattered for nearly 2,000 years.

This is the hand of God in history!

When God declared in Isaiah 46:9–10 that He alone knows all of history, He was making a sweeping statement. His declaration in part was that the Jewish people would, in the very end times, be re-gathered and brought back into the land. And in Isaiah 66:8, we read another remarkable prophecy, that in a moment, a nation would be born:

> Who has ever heard of such things? Who has ever
> seen things like this? Can a country be born in a day or
> a nation be brought forth in a moment? Yet no sooner is
> Zion in labor than she gives birth to her children (NIV).

"In a moment" Zion is brought into existence!

Independence Hall/Tel Aviv— the room where David Ben-Gurion read Israel's declaration of independence on May 14, 1948

An important consideration to think about is seen in four bullet points, so that we can know for sure we are living in the end times:

- We see the re-gathering of the Jewish people into their ancestral homeland.

- We are also the generation seeing a giant technological explosion that will allow for the fulfillment of numerous prophecies (and Israel is at the forefront of these tech advances).

- We are dealing with rogue terror nations, most of whom threaten Israel and are in pursuit of weapons of mass destruction.

- We have seen incredible apostasy in the Church of Jesus Christ; in many cases now, even evangelical leaders are refusing to stand with Israel, or they overtly stand with the Palestinians.

The key to seeing through a biblical lens in order to understand where we are in God's eternal plan is understanding the role the nation of Israel plays in the last days. This is primary.

There is also another important point, especially in dealing with critics of the "ingathering" prophetic passages. It is often said by Preterists (those who believe most of the end times prophecies were fulfilled — hold onto to your hat — in A.D. 70). They will argue that the famous "return" of the Jews actually occurred when the exiles came back from the Babylonian captivity — an event handled in some detail by prophets like Jeremiah.

And yet . . .

In Isaiah 11:11–12, we read that God intends to extend His hand the *second time*. The first time would indeed have been in the sixth century B.C., the return from Babylonian exile.

> And it shall come to pass in that day, that the Lord shall set his hand again the *second time* to recover the remnant of his people, which shall be left, from Assyria,

A stone wall from the time of the Babylonian invasion, 586 B.C.

and from Egypt, and from Pathros, and from Cush, and from Elam, and from Shinar, and from Hamath, and from the islands of the sea. And he shall set up an ensign for the nations, and shall assemble the outcasts *of Israel,* and *gather together the dispersed of Judah from the four corners of the earth* (emphasis added).

The all-important second return has occurred in the era in which we live. This is stunning.

God also declared that He would raise a banner for the nations of the world. He would assemble the scattered people of *Judah*. Note the precision of the Word of God. Never in history have Israel *and Judah* been re-gathered. On the death of Solomon, ten of the tribes of *Israel* were in the north. Judah and Benjamin, in the south, were called *Judah*. Under David and Solomon, the Jews had a united kingdom. From that time, they are referred to as Israel and Judah.

We now had a divided kingdom.

We don't have a biblical record of the northern tribes returning specifically, but we do have a record in 536 B.C. of Judah gathered and returned to their land.

This is the full record of the first return, and, as we've said, we are now witnessing the final return.

A People Without a Land

In 1894, the Viennese-born Jewish journalist and playwright, Theodor Herzl, covered a dramatic trial in Paris — that of the Jewish officer Alfred Dreyfus.

What would come to be known as "The Dreyfus Affair" would become a chilling milestone for the Jewish people in Europe, who slowly began to see that the supernaturally driven anti-Semitism would haunt them seemingly forever.

Dreyfus, a French artillery officer, was tried on trumped-up charges of treason. He was accused of passing artillery parts on to the Germans. Dreyfus was convicted.

He was sentenced to serve time at the infamous Devil's Island, and as Jews have done for millennia in the countries where they have been exiled, Dreyfus professed his allegiance to the state:

> I swear that I am innocent. I remain worthy of serving in the Army. Long live France! Long live the Army![3]

Fascinating Fact

Benjamin Disraeli served as Prime Minister of Great Britain twice: 1868, 1874–80.

By H. Lenthall
via Wikimedia Commons

Though Dreyfus was eventually exonerated, the whole incident stayed with Herzl. With that, the wheel of history began to turn in Herzl's mind, and he set about doing what he could to bring the Jews to safety. In his astounding story, we see the unfolding drama in how God's hand works in history.

During the course of that trial, Herzl began to realize that there would never be a place where Jewish people could be safe — unless, unless it was in a country of their own! No doubt Herzl pondered the words he had read so many times. Words spoken in 1853 at the end of the Crimean War fought over the rights to Palestine. Words spoken by a Jewish man who would later become world-famous. His name? Benjamin Disraeli. His words? "You ask me what I wish: my answer is a national existence, which we have not. You ask me what I wish: my answer is the Land of Promise. You ask me what I wish: my answer is, the temple, all we have forfeited, all we have yearned after, all for which we have fought, our beauteous country, our holy creed, our simple manners, and our ancient customs."[4]

The dream lived! God was miraculously at work but the process was slow.

3. https://en.wikipedia.org/wiki/Alfred_Dreyfus.

4. https://www.jewishvirtuallibrary.org/jsource/anti-semitism/Dreyfus.html.

By 1897, through extraordinary effort, Herzl organized the First Zionist Congress in Basel, Switzerland.

When the conference was over, several things came about: a national anthem (the Hatikva); a flag (with the broad blue stripes we see today flying over the state of Israel); and Herzl reiterated a statement that seems to have originated a half-century earlier with a Christian clergyman named Alexan-

Theodor Herzl
(Shutterstock)

der Keith: "There is a land without a people. There is a people without a land. It is time to give the people without a land the land without a people."[5]

It became obvious to some that the Jews believed God would give them the land from which they had been dispersed. Herzl said at the Zionist Conference that he believed it would happen within 50 years. He missed his prediction by a mere year!

Although many of the early Jews who advocated for a Jewish state (many after reading Herzl's landmark book, *The Jewish State*) were secularists, the prophesied biblical return began to stir in many a breast.

Following this historic gathering in Basel, Herzl went to work attempting to secure approval from the Turkish Sultan himself who controlled Palestine.

G. Frederick Owen writes concerning this meeting:

> For months he sought privilege of a personal interview with this grand ruler. Then one day while Herzl sat waiting in the outer office, one of the sultans many slaves entered and beckoned the distinguished looking man to follow him. They walked through the long and spacious corridors and finally arrived at the throne room. The room was decorated with many precious gems, and the

5. Ibid.

Sultan's throne was of pure gold. Tall, dignified, handsome Theodore Herzl made a low, respectful bow and began to speak as only Herzl could speak.

The Jews, he said, were persecuted everywhere in Europe, and could not seem to find a home anywhere but in America, which could not take them all. Would the Sultan consider letting them return to Palestine, their ancient homeland? While the small, round, gorgeously clothed Sultan sat on the soft pillows on his golden throne and listened, he was sufficiently impressed with his tall, handsome, eloquent visitor that he decorated him for his personal heroism and offered to permit the Jews to return to Palestine for twenty million dollars.[6]

Herzl did not have 20 million nor could he get it. His thoughts turned to the possibility of another location for the Jewish state, but God would never allow this because it would invalidate His Word!

Over the centuries, many, many Jews who had carved out lives in nations of their exile had settled down and the prospect of building a nation in the then-backwater of Palestine held no appeal. But there was also a group of people who decided to filter back into the land of Israel.

God was very much at work!

The early bands of pioneers were coming back and buying parcels, much of it malaria-infested swamps, from the Turks who would sell it because it held little to no value to them. Jews would dig ditches and drain the swamps, planting eucalyptus trees, and developing the "kibbutz" system (a collective community based on security and agriculture) of communities. As time progressed, the world found

> **Fascinating Fact**
>
> It's interesting to note that many secularists in the years following the 1st Zionist conference advocated for a Jewish state in places like Uganda as opposed to Israel because they felt the Turks would never relent. They forgot that the God that promises is the God that provides!

6. https://www.jewishvirtuallibrary.org/jsource/anti-semitism/Dreyfus.html.

itself thrust into world war. Amid
that drama, the Jews played their role
again.

In the period from 1914 to
1917, Chaim Weizmann developed
a much-needed ingredient (acetone,
a key component in gun powder) for
the British.

Partly as a thank you to the
Jewish people, the British released
what became known in 1917 as the
"Balfour Declaration" which read, in
part:

Chaim Weizmann
(Library of Congress)

> His Majesty's government views with favor the estab-
> lishment in Palestine of a national home for the Jewish
> people, and will use their best endeavors to facilitate the
> achievement of this object, it being clearly understood
> that nothing shall be done which may prejudice the civil
> and religious rights of existing non-Jewish communities
> in Palestine, or the rights and political status enjoyed by
> Jews in any other country.

Thus, one of the world's most important superpowers agreed to the establishment of a Jewish state on land that
was once Israel.

As all people are, the Jewish people
became pawns in international drama,
and as the horrors of World War I
receded, a new menace emerged: iron-
ically, a Vienna-born wanderer known
as Adolf Hitler.

Hitler believed he could restore
German pride, and so began to thumb

General Allenby's entrance
into Jerusalem
(Library of Congress)

his nose at the Versailles Treaty, which had drastically limited Germany's ability to field an army.

The brutal years between 1933 and 1945 have been well documented, so we can pick up our story in the months and years just after the fall of Nazi Germany.

As a result of the satanically driven Holocaust — the Nazi campaign to murder every single Jew — the world realized that the Jewish people must have their own homeland.

Not coincidentally, a number of new countries popped up in the Middle East, as the conquering Allied powers re-drew the maps. Kuwait, Transjordan, Iraq, and others were established, and would be in their historic place to threaten the Jewish state soon enough.

Truman and the Jews

It is a fact that God has a habit of putting the right person in the right place at the right time to bring His purposes to pass.

So it was that a failed businessman from the American Midwest took his place in the divine drama.

Though Franklin Delano Roosevelt was a beloved American president, he was passively anti-Semitic. He exerted little effort to stop the slaughter of Jews in Europe. In preparing to run for his fourth term, he was saddled with a vice presidential candidate he clearly disliked, Harry S. Truman. In fact, it is thought that FDR and the Baptist from Independence, Missouri, had only one real conversation prior to the election of 1945.

Then, without warning, on April 12, 1945, FDR died at his summer home in Warm Springs, Georgia.

All of a sudden, his vice president assumed command of the most powerful country on earth.

Timeline to May 14, 1948

- Truman once went into the clothing business with a partner named Eddie Jacobson, a Jew. They became fast friends. During slow times at their Kansas City store,

Eddie would teach Harry what God said about promises to the Jews. He taught him the great prophecies. This would later prove to be a critical element in the establishment of Israel.

- By 1947, as the Jews of Palestine were preparing to seize their moment, George Marshall, the brilliant chief of staff during World War II, and the architect of the famed plan to rebuild Europe, whispered to Truman that he ought not meddle in Middle East flashpoints by recognizing the Jews. Truman revered him. Marshall told his boss: Don't have anything to do with this new Jewish state. It's a lose-lose proposition. Truman's entire cabinet agreed!

- On May 14, 1948, as David Ben-Gurion, Golda Meir, and 350 others gathered in Tel Aviv, it was 10 a.m. in Washington D.C.

The setting for this drama could not have been more momentous:

On the day the British Mandate over Palestine expired — Friday, May 14, 1948 — the Jewish People's Council gathered at the Tel Aviv Museum to declare the establishment of the State of Israel. There is no record of who attended the meeting, but 350 invitations were sent out instructing the recipients to keep the information secret. Word got out, however, and people started singing Hatikvah in the streets even before David Ben-Gurion began reading the declaration he had written. The ceremony was held at 4 p.m. local time before the British left to avoid making the declaration on Shabbat. It took 17 minutes to read the entire document in a 32-minute ceremony. Some people signed the declaration later and one person signed twice. Four hours later, Egypt bombed Tel Aviv. The new state was recognized that night by the United States and three days later by the USSR.[7]

_____

7. http://www.jewishvirtuallibrary.org/jsource/History/Dec_of_Indep.html.

This Government has been informed that a Jewish
state has been proclaimed in Palestine, and recognition
has been requested by the *provisional* Government thereof.

The United States recognizes the provisional government as the de facto authority of the new *State of*

Israel.

Harry Truman

Approved,
May 14, 1948.

It took Truman only 11 minutes to recognize this new nation!

And so it was that the Jewish people had a toehold of a state, in the volatile Middle East. But. . . .

The Arabs went to war the next day, against the newly established state of Israel. The headlines were ominous:

Tel Aviv Is Bombed

Indeed, Egypt bombed the Israeli coastal city, and all the countries 650,000 inhabitants were in danger.

For your consideration, especially if you are wondering whether God works in the affairs of men: During the 1948–49 War of Independence, Israel had at its disposal *3,600 submachine guns,; a few leaky ships as a navy; 10,000 rifles with about 50 rounds each;*[8] French rifles that could be fired twice and then you'd have to plunge into a bucket of water in order to cool them down.

---

8. Dr. Harold L. Willmington, *Willmington's Guide to the Bible* (Wheaton, IL: Tyndale House Publishers, Inc., 1981), p. 978.

The British General Montgomery said, "Israel is a long and narrow land, impossible to defend." He also stated as he surveyed the land just prior to the 1948 declaration, "there is no way the tiny Jewish nation can survive."[9]

Hadj Amin Al Husseini, the Muslim's Grand Mufti of Jerusalem, as well as other Arab leaders, encouraged followers to kill the Jews and drive them into the sea.

The Israel Defense Forces during the 1948–49 War of Independence

The War of Independence — The Fight to Survive

By the time 1948 rolled around, there were some 650,000 Jews living in the land, surrounded by 45–50 million Muslim Arabs. On May 15, 1948, Egypt, Jordan, Iraq, Syria, and Lebanon invaded the re-born country of Israel.

When Israel declared its independence in May 1948, the army did not have a single cannon or tank. Its air force consisted of nine obsolete planes. Although the Haganah had 60,000 trained fighters, only 18,900 were fully mobilized, armed, and prepared for war.[10] On the eve of the war, David Ben-Gurion called in his two best military minds for a final assessment: Yigael

9. The Arabs in soldiers outnumbered the Jews 40 to 1, in population, 100 to 1, in equipment, 1,000 to 1, and in area, 5,000 to 1. Just prior to the war, British Field Marshall Montgomery visited Palestine and sadly predicted it would take the Arabs but eight days to drive the Jews into the sea. Their land was awkward and difficult to protect, being long and narrow with 600 miles of land frontiers, all bordering on hostile Arab states. Harold L. Willmington, *Wilmington's Guide to the Bible* (Tyndale House Publishers), p. 978.

10. Larry Collins and Dominique Lapierre, *O Jerusalem!* (NY: Simon and Schuster, 1972), p. 352.

Yadin, who was the Haganah's chief of operations, and Yisrael Galili, who was its *de facto* commander-in-chief. Their answers were both identical and terrifying. "The best we can tell you is that we have a fifty-fifty chance."[11] But God. . . .

This would be a fight for survival. The Jews knew it, and while they did not want it, they knew it could not be avoided. History has revealed that men will fight harder to protect their families than they will to expand their territory, and such was the case in 1947–49.

World War II had come to an end in Europe. America and her Allies celebrated the victory. However, for many it was a sober and horrifying discovery that would no doubt change the lives of many. Then Supreme Allied Commander and soon to be the 34th president of the United States, Dwight Eisenhower made the decision to visit personally as many of the Nazi death camps as feasible for the purpose of filming the atrocities committed by Hitler's murderers. Eisenhower, anticipating a time when these atrocities would be denied, was resolved never to let that happen. The

General of the Army Dwight D. Eisenhower, 1947

result: over 6,000 feet of film shot providing irrefutable evidence! This footage would be introduced into evidence at the war crimes trials at Nuremberg, Germany, on November 29, 1945. Astounding as it may seem, many today deny this ever happened, even though Eisenhower himself is clearly seen in much of the footage.

---

11. Golda Meir, *My Life* (London: Futura Publications, 1975), p. 181.

The result of this attempt to simply eradicate an entire ethnicity actually ended up being used by God to move the hearts and minds of the newly formed United Nations, birthed October 24, 1945.

Together, these civilized nations came together on November 29, 1947, to issue U.N. Resolution 181, better known as the "Partition Plan."

God was ramping up His plan to restore the Jews to the land He had given them, but whose usage had been lost due to their disobedience. The Jews gladly accepted the resolution; however, their Arab neighbors rejected it out of hand and called for war!

But what was God doing behind the scenes? How was He at work and in what arenas was He busily moving about to fulfill His plan?

The Jewish state was going to come into existence! How could this happen with so little military equipment and trained personnel against such overwhelming odds?

The United States had passed the Neutrality Act of 1935, which in essence banned any American from aiding in any foreign conflict. This had transpired due to America's isolationist policies propagated by President Woodrow Wilson.[12]

This was a real problem because there were many American Jews who felt compelled to aid Israel in their War of Independence.

In 1948, just three years after the liberation of Nazi death camps, a group of American Jewish pilots answered a call for help. In secret and at great personal risk, they smuggled planes out of the U.S., trained behind the Iron Curtain in Czechoslovakia, and flew for Israel in its War of Independence. Their stories have been chronicled in a documentary titled *Above and Beyond* by Nancy Spielberg, sister of famed movie mogul Steven Spielberg.

As members of the Machal (or Mahal) — "volunteers from abroad" — this ragtag band of brothers not only turned the tide

---

12. For details, see http://20012009.state.gov/r/pa/ho/time/id/99849.htm.

of the war but also embarked on personal journeys of discovery and renewed Jewish pride.

These were men like Al Schwimmer, who is regarded by many as the father of the Israeli Air Force. Schwimmer worked for the now-defunct TWA airline and was a flight engineer for the U.S. Air Transport Command in World War II. Upon learning of the need for aircraft for the new nation of Israel, he smuggled 30 surplus planes to the Jewish state in 1948. He also recruited pilots and crewmembers from the U.S.

After the war, Schwimmer was indicted for violating the U.S. Neutrality Act and lost his citizenship. He stayed in Israel and founded Israel Aerospace Industries. In 2001, he was pardoned by U.S. President Bill Clinton.

The pilots featured in *Above and Beyond* are Leon Frankel, Coleman Goldstein, Lou Lenart, George Lichter, Gideon Lichtman, Harold Livingston, Milton Rubenfeld, Smoky Simon, Stan Andrews, and Bob Vickman. Art students at University of California–Los Angeles in 1948, Andrews and Vickman had been stationed in the Pacific with the U.S. Air Force in World War II. They arrived in Israel in June 1948. In a Tel Aviv bar, they created the logo for the 101 Squadron unit of the Israeli Air Force, scribbling the "Angel of Death" insignia on a cocktail napkin. Their design is still on Israeli F-16 jets today. Both men were killed when their planes were shot down in separate incidents in July and October 1948.

With the exception of Lenart, whose family members were recent immigrants to the U.S. at the time, the pilots were all second-generation Americans. They were part of the group of American Jews who had come from Eastern Europe and other places in the first quarter of the 20th century. [13]

However, it wasn't just flyboys who engaged! Enter Colonel David Marcus. David Daniel "Mickey" Marcus, a tough Brooklyn

---

13. http://jewishexponent.com/headlines/2015/04/the-american-pilots-who-fought-for-israel-in-1948.

street kid, rose by virtue of his courage and intelligence to help save Israel in 1948 and become its first general since Judah Maccabee. After a distinguished career in military and public service to the United States, the 46-year-old Marcus wrote his name forever in the annals of Israeli history.

In 1944, Marcus's consciousness of himself as a Jew took a dramatic turn when he was put in charge of planning how to sustain the starving millions in the regions liberated by the Allied invasion of Europe. A major part of his responsibilities involved clearing out the Nazi death camps. Here, Marcus came face to face with the survivors of Nazi atrocities and saw with his own eyes the piles of uncounted Jewish corpses in Europe's death camps.

Following that assignment, Marcus was named chief of the War Crimes Division, planning legal and security procedures for the Nuremberg trials. Through these experiences, Marcus came to understand the depths of European anti-Semitism. Though never previously a Zionist, Marcus became convinced that the only hope for the remnants of European Jewry lay in a Jewish homeland in Palestine.

In 1947, Marcus returned to civilian life. A few months later, the United Nations authorized the partition of Palestine and the eventual creation of a Jewish state. Within days, David Ben-Gurion asked Marcus to recruit an American officer to serve as military advisor to Israel. Failing in his attempts to recruit one of his friends, Marcus decided to volunteer himself. The U.S. War Department granted Marcus, who was a reservist, permission to accept the offer, provided Marcus not use his own name or rank and disguise his military record.

Thus, one "Michael Stone" arrived in Tel Aviv in January 1948, to confront a nearly impossible situation. The widely separated Jewish settlements in Palestine were surrounded by a sea of hostile Arabs. The newly created Israel would have no defensible borders, no air power, a few tanks and ancient artillery pieces, and almost no arms or ammunition. The Haganah was an effective underground organization, but it had no experience as a regular national army. Facing it were well-supplied Arab armies determined to drive the Jews into the sea. The pro-Arab British administration in Palestine prevented the importation of military supplies to the Israelis.

Undaunted, Stone designed a command structure for Israel's new army and wrote manuals to train it, adapting his experience at Ranger school to the Haganah's special needs. He identified Israel's weakest points as the scattered settlements in the Negev and the new quarter of Jerusalem. When Israel declared independence and the Arab armies attacked in May 1948, Israel was ready, thanks to Stone's planning. His hit-and-run tactics kept the Egyptian army in the Negev off balance. When the Jewish section of Jerusalem was about to fall, Marcus ordered the construction of a road to bring additional men and equipment to break the Arab siege just days before the United Nations negotiated a ceasefire. Israel had withstood the Arab assault with its borders virtually intact.

In gratitude, Ben-Gurion named Marcus a lieutenant general, the first general in the army of Israel in nearly two thousand years.

Tragically, Marcus did not live to see the peace. Six hours before the ceasefire began, in the village of Abu Ghosh near Jerusalem, Marcus was unable to sleep. He walked beyond the guarded perimeter wrapped in his bed sheet. A Jewish sentry saw a white-robed figure approaching and, not understanding Marcus's response, fired a single, fatal shot. Marcus's body was flown back for burial at West Point, where his tombstone identifies him as "A Soldier for All Humanity." Hollywood would later immortalize Marcus in a movie, *Cast a Giant Shadow*.

Ben-Gurion put it simply, "He was the best man we had."[14]

And there were more, many more, who were moved to go and fight! Why do we write their stories? Because God works through

14. https://www.jewishvirtuallibrary.org/jsource/biography/marcus.html.

people! People just like us, just like you, if we allow Him! By the way, we urge you to rent or stream it via YouTube, and watch the movie mentioned above: *Cast a Giant Shadow* with Kirk Douglas, John Wayne, and Frank Sinatra! Great investment of a couple of hours!

Nothing was going to prohibit the prophecies from coming to pass. Israel won. The years would pass, and Israel would not only survive, but thrive.

- They won the 1956 Suez War against ancient nemesis Egypt.

- The Six Day War in June of 1967 secured the biblical homeland on the mountains of Israel and liberated biblical Judea and Samaria.

- The Yom Kippur War in 1973, also a victory, was so miraculous (Israel was caught completely off-guard by Egypt and Syria) that one struggles to explain Israel's hard-won victory without acknowledging the hand of the Lord.

The Lord, you see, not only promised to restore them to the land, but also to protect them in the land.

Consider: During the October 1973 Yom Kippur War, Israel's enemies had at their disposal 5,000 tanks, more than the combined tanks of Britain and France in WWII! In fact, during those tense three weeks in 1973, Israel was aware of their potential fate. Prime Minister Golda Meir appealed to one of her few friends, and once again an American president stepped up.

In her darkest moments, Meir phoned and reportedly said, "Mr. President, we're going to lose our country if we do not have the needed military equipment on the ground in Tel Aviv within 24 hours."

That call came at 3 a.m., and Richard Nixon took it. He gave his word that the needed equipment and munitions would be delivered within 24 hours. This despite his Joint Chiefs virtually demanding that he not comply, since they had their own issues to deal with in Vietnam.

Nixon wrote later that he sat on the edge of his bed that night and realized why he had become president. His own secretary of state, Henry Kissinger, sounded positively like Marshall a generation before: "Let the Jews bleed a little longer."

Later it would come out that Nixon's mother would sit him down and read to him from the Bible. She'd say, as reported by filmmaker Bill McKay: "Richard, the Jews are the chosen people of God. I really feel like there will come a day in your life when you can help the Jewish people. Do all that is within your power to help them."

"I promised my mother I would." Defying the Joint Chiefs and a waffling cabinet secretary, Nixon directly ordered Operation Nickel Grass to begin without delay or hesitation![15]

Israel held on and turned back the Muslim efforts to annihilate them.

Since then, two Intifadas or uprisings have been launched against Israel (this referring to the Palestinian efforts at violence); the country has fought in Lebanon two times. They are constantly being attacked by people that hate them. Yet today, Israel not only survives . . . she thrives, surrounded by enemies on three sides and the Mediterranean to the west, she survives!

William F. Albright, professor of Semitic languages at Johns Hopkins University, expressed his wonder at the rebirth of Israel. He wrote: "No other phenomenon in history is quite so extraordinary as the unique event represented by the Restoration of Israel. . . . At no other time in world history, so far as it is known, has a people been destroyed, and then come back after a lapse of time and reestablished itself. It is utterly out of the question to

---

15. Portions of this section are from investigative reporter Michael Greenspan in the made-for-TV series *Against All Odds* produced by William (Bill) McKay.

seek a parallel for the recurrence of Israel's restoration after 2,500 years of former history."[16]

God puts the right people in the right place to make the right decision in His history, time and time again.

The land belongs to them through the promise of Isaac; *the Creator God who spoke the world into existence declared it.*

This is the hand of God working in history.

In Jeremiah 29:11, God made certain specific promises to the Jewish people. If God made promises to the nation of Israel and is keeping those promises . . . my question to you is: do you think that same God can keep the promises He's made to you? Do you think you could trust a God like that, who knows the end from the beginning? Our prayer is that you can, you have, and you will continue to do so.

This gives you an overview of how all this has occurred, prophetically. We will now look at it all in some detail.

---

16. Moshe Davis, *Israel: Its Role in Civilization* (Seminary Israel Institute of the Jewish Theological Seminary of America; distributed by Harper, 1956), p. 31.

Chapter 7

Israel Today

Think of this: by 1945, the Nazis had murdered six million Jews in Europe (1.5 million were children!).

A mere three years later, the state of Israel was established.

Today, just under 7 million Jews *live* in Israel!

If you ever wonder about the existence of God, and whether He cares about you, ponder the above fact.

An Amazing Prophecy

No other people in history have been so harassed and hunted as the Jews. Apart from the biblical story, it makes no sense, even though countless answers have been provided to the heartfelt question, "Why?"

From the time of Abraham to now, the Jews have been targets of violence all over the world. Tragically, as we saw in the speech of Israeli Prime Minister Benjamin Netanyahu in 2015, the world is silent about this violence, this Jew-hatred — even when a nation like Iran openly calls for Israel's destruction.

The world continues to do business with the oil-rich Muslim dictatorship!

Preeminent on people's minds today, where Israel is concerned, is the race Iran is running to obtain nuclear weapons. This is perhaps the greatest existential threat to Israel in its history.

And yet . . .

In Isaiah 54:17, we read:

> No weapon that is formed against thee shall prosper; and every tongue that shall rise against thee in judgment thou shalt condemn. This is the heritage of the servants of the LORD, and their righteousness is of me, saith the LORD.

This is absolutely amazing, given the attempts to exterminate the Jewish people. Just one example of the continual fulfillment of this prophecy came in the summer of 1981.

Saddam Hussein, the brutal ruler of Iraq (and at the time, a client of the United States), conceived of a "super gun" that could launch nuclear warheads directly at Israel.

By early June, the director of Israel's Mossad intelligence community came to Prime Minister Menachem Begin and told the PM that Iraq's nuclear reactor at Osirak would soon "go hot" and that would be the point of no return.

Begin thought about it and ordered eight fighter jets to bomb the reactor in Iraq! Adding tension to an already epic moment, he didn't first phone U.S. President Ronald Reagan, thus giving Israel the greatest element of surprise. The Israelis, after all, face *existential threats*, unlike other nations. If Israel loses just once, they disappear.

On the day of the attack, Israel's war planners wanted the strike force to go in at night, but Col. Ze'ev Raz argued that his pilots had to attack in broad daylight, so that they could site the target clearly. This placed the already extraordinary operation even more in peril.

But remember Isaiah 54:17. The Israeli pilots dropped 16 two-ton bombs on Osirak; 14 were a direct hit, and the planes returned home safely.

As they flew due west, Raz noticed the sun on the horizon. He radioed back and each pilot recited in unison:

> *Sun, stand still over Gibeon, and you, moon, over the Valley of Aijalon.*
> *So the sun stood still, and the moon stopped, till the nation avenged itself on its enemies. . . .*

This passage, from Joshua 10:12–13, confirmed that the pilots understood the unbroken circle of feeling that they share with their ancestors. And it proved once again that prophetic Scripture is true and sure!

There are almost countless examples of the miracles that followed miracles as Israel was created out of a bleak, desert-like landscape. Let's look at some of those achievements.

The Technology Explosion

> But thou, O Daniel, shut up the words, and seal the book, even to the time of the end: many shall run to and fro, and knowledge shall be increased (Daniel 12:4).

In 2011, authors Dan Senor and Saul Singer wrote *Start-up Nation: The Story of Israel's Economic Miracle.* The book is an amazing look at the technological advances made by the Israelis, most of whom have companies headquartered in and around Tel Aviv. In less than 100 years, the area has gone from white-hot sand dunes to a "Silicon Valley" environment unmatched by any other country.

Even the secular-thinking Shimon Peres understands the roots of this incredible miracle:

> The seeds of a new Israel grew from the imagination of an exiled people. The exile was extremely long, some two thousand years. The exile left the Jews with a prayer and without a country. Yet this unbroken prayer nurtured their hope and their bond to the land of their forefathers. The hostility of the environment did not subside. Israel was attacked seven times in the first sixty-two years of its existence and subjected to comprehensive diplomatic and economic embargoes. No foreign soldiers came to its aid. The only way we could overcome our attackers' quantitative superiority of weapons was to create an advantage built on courage and technology.[1]

These technological examples are little known outside the business world, but let us ask: Do you use a cellphone? Do you have a computer? Chances are, the core technology used in the machines was developed by an Israeli in Israel.

In *Start-up Nation*, Senor and Singer give scores of examples, including that of innovator Jon Medved:

> In his presentations he says only half-jokingly that if Israel followed the lead of "Intel Inside" — Intel's marketing campaign to highlight the ubiquity of its chips — with similar "Israel Inside" stickers, they would show up on almost everything people around the world touch, and he ticks off a litany of examples: from computers, to cell phones, to medical devices and miracle drugs, to Internet-based social networks, to cutting-edge sources of clean energy, to the food we eat, to the registers in the supermarkets in which we shop.[2]

---

1. Dan Senor and Saul Singer, *Start-up Nation: The Story of Israel's Economic Miracle* (New York: Grand Central Publishing), kindle edition, 9/7/2011, p. xii.
2. Ibid., p. 65.

Marcella Rosen, who heads the New York-based *Untold News,* uncovers stories of Israeli innovations in the fields of technology, medicine, and agriculture. Rosen even wrote a book, *Tiny Dynamo*, a quick little read filled with big stories of innovations. For example, Israeli doctors and hospitals welcome even Palestinian patients and provide life-saving treatment.

The Israelis also are continuously developing technology to make lives better around the world. Witness their unique research into water shortages, and the work of Yoram Oren, who manages Ben-Gurion University's Department of Desalination & Water Treatment, seeks to separate salt from seawater, thus providing adequate quantities of fresh water for people who live in parched lands:

> "Nature seeks equilibrium," he says. "Desalination, separating the salt from sea water to make fresh water, is an act of overcoming what nature is seeking. It's not easy."[3]

Another Israeli researcher, Sidney Loeb, developed a system in the 1960s that could help with desalination. Oren and others work from Loeb's development of a semi-permeable membrane that aids the cause:

> The new methodology involves much in the way of advance electro-chemical engineering, but suffice to say that the method took off, and according to Prof. Oren, it's recognized around the world as the most advanced, efficient way of freshening seawater in use today. And we should hope that the trend toward Prof. Loeb's methodology continues.[4]

What are these kinds of developments if not part of the fulfillment of Bible prophecy?

In Isaiah 27:6, we read:

---

3. http://untoldnews.org/desalination/.
4. Ibid.

He shall cause them that come of Jacob to take root: Israel shall blossom and bud, and fill the face of the world with fruit.

A few chapters later, the same theme:

The wilderness and the solitary place shall be glad for them; and the desert shall rejoice, and blossom as the rose (Isaiah 35:1).

Mark Twain wrote in his report on traveling through Palestine:

Come to Galilee for that . . . these unpeopled deserts, these rusty mounds of barrenness, that never, never do shake the glare from their harsh outlines, and fade and faint into vague perspective; that melancholy ruin of Capernaum: this stupid village of Tiberias, slumbering under its six funereal palms. . . . We reached Tabor safely. . . . We never saw a human being on the whole route.

Nazareth is forlorn. . . . Jericho the accursed lies a moldering ruin today, even as Joshua's miracle left it

The ancient synagogue in Capernaum, where Jesus taught

more than three thousand years ago: Bethlehem and Bethany, in their poverty and their humiliation, have nothing about them now to remind one that they once knew the high honor of the Savior's presence; the hallowed spot where the shepherds watched their flocks by night, and where the angels sang, "Peace on earth, good will to men," is untenanted by any living creature. . . . Bethsaida and Chorzin have vanished from the earth, and the "desert places" round about them, where thousands of men once listened to the Savior's voice and ate the miraculous bread, sleep in the hush of a solitude that is inhabited only by birds of prey and skulking foxes.[5]

That Palestine had become a ruinous heap after the Roman expulsion of the Jews in the second century is well documented. The land became like a moonscape. That makes Israel's "reclamation project" all the more incredible.

We have been to Israel many times, and the explosion of innovation never ceases to amaze. One of the greatest scenes comes into view in the south, near the Dead Sea.

When one drives down the highway, startling scenes start to emerge: palm groves. On either side of the highway, Israeli researchers have planted and cultivate dozens of large-scale palm groves, working to reclaim the barrenness of the Judean Hills.

Recalling the verses from Isaiah above, did you know that Israel exports more tulips than Holland? Or did you know that the country's *shuks* (vegetable markets) are bulging with huge, delicious vegetables and fruits? Truly, Israel is blooming like a rose in a desert.

The Israel Defense Forces

Another fulfillment of prophecy is the presence of an army that is feared the world over, especially in the Middle East.

---

5. http://www.eretzyisroel.org/~peters/depopulated.html.

In the "Dry Bones" prophecy found in Ezekiel 37, God alludes to the presence of an end-times army in Israel:

> So I prophesied as he commanded me, and the breath came into them, and they lived, and stood up upon their feet, an exceeding great army (Ezekiel 37:10).

Another reference is found in Zechariah 14:14, where we read "And Judah also shall fight at Jerusalem," and the Lord Himself will fight ahead of the army, as He did in ancient times.

The IDF began as a defense force in the kibbutz a century ago, and by World War II was being developed into a first-rate fighting force.

Let us take a look at some of the miraculous modern moments involving this "Army of the Lord."

June 1967

Nineteen years after statehood, as the Jews were building a modern state that brought culture and innovation to the region like never before, their Arab enemies were still obsessed with getting rid of Israel.

By the spring of 1967, Egypt's dictator, Gamal Abdel Nasser, expelled U.N. peacekeepers in the Sinai, and massed troops on his border with Israel.

In the north, Nasser's ally, Syria, was prepared to pour over the strategic Golan Heights.

To the east, a waffling king, Hussein, was warned by Israel to stay out of any possible conflict, but his signed pact with Nasser compelled him to attack.

One element in the long lead-up to what would come to be known as the Six Day War boggles the mind when we remember God's promises of miracles and provision for His people in times of trouble.

For a decade before the June '67 war, Israel's Ezer Weizman was chief of the air force. He began to develop a component of future war plans that would prove to be critical. In those days, the Egyptians were a client state (what a dramatic fall from their ancient status) of the Soviet Union. Russian MiG fighters and other military equipment were in the land of the Pharaohs, and Nasser intended to use them in a war of extermination. He said as much.

Into this environment operated an Israeli prime minister, Levi Eshkol, who was anything but forceful and reassuring. He certainly felt the weight of his people's survival on his shoulders. Fortunately for him, he was served by Israel's brilliant Chief of Staff, Yitzhak Rabin, and others, like Weizman.

It was Weizman's idea to get the upper hand on the Soviet-backed Egyptian Air Force. Code-named "Focus," the operation called for Israel to reduce its turnaround time for pilots (bombing run, return to base, and refuel and rearm for another go), because for Israel, a tiny country in a sea of enemies, there is no margin for error and every minute counts. Incredibly, Israel's air force crews reduced the turnaround time to . . . eight minutes.

Egypt never knew what hit her.

Michael Oren details the plan in his book, *Six Days of War:*

> All but twelve of the country's jets were thrown into the attack — American football fans would call it a Hail Mary — leaving the country's skies virtually defenseless. Innumerable practice runs had convinced IAF commanders that the Egyptian air force could be destroyed, even if it managed to get off the runways, in as little as three hours.[6]

On the morning of Monday, June 5, Israel launched a preemptive strike:

> Sweating, guzzling pitchers of water — "like a giant radiator," Weizman observed — Hod waited for news of the opening wave of attack. The lead formations had

---

6. Michael Oren, *Six Days of War* (New York: RosettaBooks), kindle edition, 7/1/2010, kindle locations 4257–4258.

now passed over the sea where, using electronic jamming equipment, they were able to elude detection by Soviet vessels. At 7:30 Israel time, the first targets came into view. In the huge bases of Fa'id and Kibrit, for example, which Egyptian intelligence had erroneously concluded were out of Israel's range, the jets were parked on the aprons, in rows or in semicircular revetments. Many airfields had only one runway — block it and the planes supposed to use it were doomed.[7]

Nasser was about to experience the same thoughts that tortured the Pharaoh of the Exodus:

The jets dove. They approached in foursomes and attacked in pairs, each making three passes — four, if time permitted — the first for bombing and the rest to strafe. Priority was to be given to destroying the runways, then to the long-range bombers that threatened Israeli cities, and then to the jet fighters, the MiG's. Last to be raided were missile, radar, and support facilities. Each sortie was to take between seven and ten minutes. With a twenty-minute return flight, an eight-minute refueling time, and ten minutes' rest for the pilot, the planes would be in action again well within an hour. During that hour, moreover, the Egyptian bases would be under almost uninterrupted attack.[8]

The result was that the IAF knocked out half the Egyptian Air Force within the first 30 minutes of the war! The rest of the week was in effect a "cleanup" operation, and with Israel defeating Egypt, Jordan, and Syria simultaneously, all of a sudden control of the biblical landscape came into view.

By June 10, Israel was in possession of the Sinai Peninsula (where Moses and the children of Israel had wandered),

---

7. Ibid., kindle Locations 4269–4274.
8. Ibid., kindle Location 4281.

the strategic Golan Heights, and most important emotionally, the "mountains of Israel," including the Old City of Jerusalem. Now, they were back for all time, in fulfillment of scores of prophecies.

For 2,000 years, since the reign of the Maccabees had come to an end, Jews the world over had prayed for a return to the Holy City. Now they had control of all of Judea, Samaria, and the entire Old City with the Wailing Wall. As the soldiers broke through into the walled city they ran to the Wailing Wall and there they prayed for the first time in 2,000 years! But then, Moshe Dayan, Minister of Defense, made a tragic mistake. In an effort to appease the Muslims he granted them control of Temple Mount, the 35 acres on the heights of Mount Moriah where the Temple had once stood and where the Muslim Dome of the Rock has been since 687. While the act was intended to appease, the unintended consequence has been tragic in that Jews are harassed and limited in their access to this holy site.

Yom Kippur 1973

A mere half-dozen years after the miracle of '67, Israel was somewhat complacent, not believing her immediate neighbors were an existential threat. A threat, yes, but after their shattering defeat in the previous decade, they wouldn't dare try it again. That tragic miscalculation cost the state of Israel 2,500 dead in the fall of 1973.

Yom Kippur is the holiest day on the Jewish calendar. It marks the day that collectively and individually the nation of Israel considers the sins of the previous year. A visitor during Yom Kippur, for example in the more secular city of Tel Aviv, will see that truly the nation comes together as one. For 24 hours, not even a car moves on the roads.

On October 6, 1973, Israelis were at home with their families. Ariel Sharon, considered to be Israel's version of America's General Patton, had retired the previous spring and was home on his farm.

By sundown, the phone rang. Sharon was informed that a twin surprise attack, led by Egypt and Syria, had left Israel terribly vulnerable. With Syrian tanks pouring over the Golan, and 1,000 Egyptian T-72 tanks (again supplied by the Soviets), Israeli positions were overrun.

In the Middle East, wars usually don't last for years, and the 1973 conflict was no exception. Within the first 24 hours of the war, Israeli leaders like Moshe Dayan were gloomily predicting the end of the state.

Meanwhile, Sharon had raced to the southern front, in the Sinai, and was coordinating operations there. With years of experience, going back to brutal fighting at Latrun in 1948, Sharon had specific ideas about how to defeat the Arabs. One was his belief that while the Arabs were excellent at executing a specific plan, they lacked an ability to adapt to changes in the war.

It was this weakness that Sharon worked to exploit. He hatched a plan (well into the war) to cross the Suez Canal at night, and cut off Egyptian tanks and artillery. Still playing catch-up, his superiors ignored him for a time.

But soon they needed him.

It was at 1:35 a.m. in the early hours of October 16 that the first Israeli troops crossed the Suez Canal. Within seven hours a three-mile bridgehead had been established.[9]

By mid-morning, Sharon's forces had completely encircled Egypt's Third Army. In the north, Israel tank units were within an hour of Damascus. All of a sudden, Israel had completely reversed the realities of the war, and the Arabs again went down to a demoralizing defeat. Israel was outnumbered six to one during the war. What explains their miraculous victory?

You know *Who* explains it!

---

9. Martin Gilbert, *Israel: A History* (New York: RosettaBooks), 6/5/2014, kindle edition, p. 447.

Entebbe

A third military miracle occurred for Israel during America's bicentennial year, 1976.

In those days, terrorists, particularly the Arafat-led PLO, resorted to hijacking passenger jets, then making political demands. In 1972, a Sabeena airliner was stormed by Israeli commandoes (led by future prime ministers Ehud Barak and Benjamin Netanyhau).

The Israelis had experience in this area.

On Tuesday, June 29, on a routine flight from Tel Aviv to Paris, an Air France jetliner was hijacked just after refueling in Athens. A handful of PLO and German terrorists ordered the pilots to fly very far south. Finally, the plane reached its destination at a remote Ugandan airport, at Entebbe.

This particular hijacking was extremely problematic for the Israelis (of the 300 passengers onboard, 105 were Jews), mainly due to the long distance, which would prohibit a rescue operation.

Beginning in the hour after news reached Israel, the cabinet, under the leadership of Prime Minister Yitzhak Rabin, was under enormous pressure from families of the hostages.

"Do whatever they want, just bring our relatives home!" they shouted outside the prime minister's residence and the Knesset.

The terrorists wanted 58 other terrorists released from prisons in Europe and Israel. But Israel had always followed a policy of not negotiating with terrorists as had America.

Soon, though, the extraordinary circumstances virtually forced Rabin to announce that negotiations would commence. Because of this concession, the terrorists pushed back their deadline to Sunday morning, July 4.

That was all the breathing space the Israelis would need.

By the slimmest of margins, they crafted a daring rescue operation, involving flying four planeloads of commandoes 2,500 miles — at night.

While network news anchors, U.N. officials, and various capitols watched anxiously, Rabin and Defense Minister Shimon Peres dispatched 200 troops, including the 30-member strike force from Sayeret Matkal (Israel's most elite counter-terrorism unit) to Entebbe.

Under cover of darkness, precisely at midnight on July 3–4, the rescue force landed at Entebbe's airport. Driving the mile to the terminal building where the hostages were kept, the unit then stormed the building, killing all the terrorists within 90 seconds. They then loaded the stunned hostages onto the transport planes for the trip home.

One of the members of the Unit said, of that night:

> A hundred things had to go right for us; if one had failed, it would have been a disaster. Most important for us was the element of surprise. If the terrorists had known what was happening ahead of time, they would simply have begun killing the hostages.
>
> Do you know, they didn't know what was happening until I was standing in the doorway. A German terrorist was lying on the floor and fired at me first. I felt bullets and glass fly past my neck, but nothing hit me. I fired a burst and killed him.[10]

By the time the planes were back in Israeli airspace, the world was just finding out that the Israelis had done the unthinkable.

How do you think they did it?

You *know* how they did it!

Miracle, upon miracle, upon miracle.

> Then shall the LORD go forth, and fight against those nations, as when he fought in the day of battle (Zechariah 14:3).

---

10. Conversation with the authors, 2005.

Section Three

The Future

Chapter 8

God's Endgame

I f God has an endgame plan, and He does, can we know what is coming? Remember this, the ONLY reliable source for what the future holds is found in the Word of God. Man can speculate! Man can postulate! Man can even attempt to articulate! But man cannot understand what is coming, apart from the Word of God! The fact remains that most people outside of Christ are clueless and the majorities within the church are marginally better informed since so many pastors ignore Bible prophecy. We must not forget the spiritual element in understanding what is coming.

God says:

> But the natural man receiveth not the things of the Spirit of God: for they are foolishness unto him: neither can he know them, because they are spiritually discerned (1 Corinthians 2:14).

An Amazing Prophecy

In Isaiah 17, we read about a strange, end-times scenario in which Damascus — today still the oldest, continually habitable city in the world — is destroyed completely. As in "ceases to exist." Overnight!

How could this be? Let's read the pertinent passages:

The burden of Damascus. Behold, Damascus is taken away from being a city, and it shall be a ruinous heap.

The cities of Aroer are forsaken: they shall be for flocks, which shall lie down, and none shall make them afraid.

The fortress also shall cease from Ephraim, and the kingdom from Damascus, and the remnant of Syria: they shall be as the glory of the children of Israel, saith the LORD of hosts.

And in that day it shall come to pass, that the glory of Jacob shall be made thin, and the fatness of his flesh shall wax lean.

And it shall be as when the harvestman gathereth the corn, and reapeth the ears with his arm; and it shall be as he that gathereth ears in the valley of Rephaim.

Yet gleaning grapes shall be left in it, as the shaking of an olive tree, two or three berries in the top of the uppermost bough, four or five in the outmost fruitful branches thereof, saith the LORD God of Israel.

At that day shall a man look to his Maker, and his eyes shall have respect to the Holy One of Israel.

And he shall not look to the altars, the work of his hands, neither shall respect that which his fingers have made, either the groves, or the images.

In that day shall his strong cities be as a forsaken bough, and an uppermost branch, which they left because of the children of Israel: and there shall be desolation.

Because thou hast forgotten the God of thy salvation, and hast not been mindful of the rock of thy strength, therefore shalt thou plant pleasant plants, and shalt set it with strange slips:

In the day shalt thou make thy plant to grow, and in the morning shalt thou make thy seed to flourish: but the harvest shall be a heap in the day of grief and of desperate sorrow.

Woe to the multitude of many people, which make a noise like the noise of the seas; and to the rushing of nations, that make a rushing like the rushing of mighty waters!

The nations shall rush like the rushing of many waters: but God shall rebuke them, and they shall flee far off, and shall be chased as the chaff of the mountains before the wind, and like a rolling thing before the whirlwind.

And behold at eveningtide trouble; and before the morning he is not. This is the portion of them that spoil us, and the lot of them that rob us.

In the very first verse, we see that something arises that causes Damascus, Syria, to be wiped out. Then in verses 12–14, we see the "rushing" of many nations. In verse 14, the whole affair takes place overnight, beginning in the evening. By morning, both Damascus and "the nations" are no more.

We must be careful not to be dogmatic about prophecies that have not come to pass. Yet some passages are specific enough that we can make educated guesses.

Currently, Damascus, Syria, is still the capitol of that Muslim country. For decades, the Assad family has run the country like a crime syndicate. Since 2000, Bashar Assad has picked up where his father left off: a terrorist ruler friendly with Iran and the Russians. The Assads have threatened Israel for 40 years, and in today's grue-some civil war (250,000 dead in four years, and millions more fleeing), the worst possible scenarios are in focus: ISIS and other terror entities operating openly. In the fall of 2015, due to U.S. President Barack Obama's retreats in the region, Russia swept into Syria to prop up Assad.

It has been known for a long time that Russia covets a warm-weather port in the Middle East. Vladimir Putin is strong-arming his way back into the region, and none of this is good for Israel.

We know that conditions will cause Isaiah 17 to be fulfilled to the letter, and one day soon. In the 1973 Yom Kippur War, Israel's situation was so desperate that Golda Meir considered using battlefield nukes against the Syri-ans and this arsenal was housed at — are you ready — a kibbutz named Zechariah. Had the Israelis used those weapons, Isaiah 17 would have been fulfilled then.

With geopolitical conditions white-hot again, we can see the broad outlines of the destruction of Damascus taking shape!

So what looms on the horizon? Will Israel survive? Will America? How much time do we have?

There's good news and bad news. Yes, Israel will survive, but her darkest days are ahead. Yes, all Israel shall be saved in the end (Romans 11:26–27), but Zechariah tells us the bad news that is heartbreaking.

> And it shall come to pass, that in all the land, saith the LORD, two parts therein shall be cut off and die; but the third shall be left therein (Zechariah 13:8).

The Jewish people, in a state of lostness due to their continued rejection of Jesus as Messiah, will become the target for forces of evil for a period of seven years. During these 2,520 days, Satan will attempt to annihilate them, but God will not allow this. At the same time, God will judge them for their stubbornness and hardness of heart. But God! In the end of the seven years of unprecedented tribulation those, that is the one-third that survive, will turn to Jesus when they see Him coming on the clouds of Glory (Zechariah 12–13; Revelation 19:11–21; Romans 11:26–27).

God's endgame is found in numerous places in Scripture, but allow us to overview it with bullet points:

1. Jesus spoke of the sorrow or birth pains in Matthew 24:8. He makes it clear that the closer the world moves toward the consummation of history, events will take place with greater frequency and greater intensity. Like the pains associated with the birth of a child.

2. What type of events? Spiritual deception. Wars. Threats of wars. Famine. Earthquakes. Disease. Loss of love. Ethnic strife. Perversion of all kinds. Godlessness. Hatred of good and love of evil. Hatred of the Jews and Christians. Technological advances and much more!

3. The true Church of Jesus will be caught up to the Father's house to be with Christ, as He makes good on His promise that we will be where He is (John 14:1–3). Many call this the *Rapture* of the Church. Every Christian will be taken out of this world and will meet Jesus in the air (1 Thessalonians 4:16–18).

4. America's status as a friend and protector of Israel, although in a diminished state, ends with the departure of true believers opening the door for a war prophesied 2,500 years ago by Ezekiel the prophet as recorded in chapters 38–39. As I write these words, for the first time in history an anti-Israel coalition has now been formed as Scripture states. Russia (ancient Magog) has moved into Syria to

strengthen the Assad regime. Russia is facilitating Iran in their quest for nuclear weapons and systems to deliver them. The entire Middle East is in flames as ISIS marches across Iraq and Syria while the Taliban expands its reign of terror in Afghanistan. America pulls its missiles out of Turkey. All of this is aimed at annihilating Israel once and for all. But God! God intervenes and spares Israel while slaughtering their Muslim enemies on the mountains of Israel. God does in a flash what the nations of the world had been unable to do. Islam is destroyed!

5. The above-referenced slaughter is the springboard for a new call for worldwide peace and the laying down of all weapons. The world wants a leader and a group hug! Satan has a man, and he has a name. In fact he has several names, such as the Antichrist, the beast, the son of perdition, the deceiver, the man of sin, etc. His plan is to deceive the world and deceive them he does with a peace plan that solves the Jewish/Palestinian/Muslim problem. He initiates a 7-year plan for peace with a provision for the Jewish Temple to be built where the Muslim Dome of the Rock stood since 691. The Dome was destroyed by an earthquake occurring at the end of the Ezekiel war, signaling the close of Muslim domination of the Temple Mount.

6. Once the Peace Treaty (Daniel 9:24–27) is initiated, the Jews start the rebuilding of their holy temple that is vital to their theology. They believe "If we build it, He, the Messiah, will come and inhabit it." The Antichrist meanwhile begins his program of world domination, one world government under his control, and a cashless society. In the beginning he woos the masses with his charisma, but when that fails he turns to forced obedience. Meanwhile, religion continues and is led by the False Prophet, who aligns himself with the plan of the Antichrist.

A model of the Jewish Temple, Israel Museum, Jerusalem

7. In the middle of the seven biblical years, 1,260 days following the Peace Treaty, an incident takes place that gives the illusion the Antichrist has been killed. However, he then appears to be raised from the dead. We say "illusion" because this is the work of Satan. Satan can perform miracles, but he cannot raise anyone from the dead! This power is reserved for the giver of life only. This seeming resurrection proves to a deceived and blinded population that this is the Messiah, this is Jesus, this is the Muslim Mahdi, this is God! The world buys it, and why wouldn't they? That is, except for a growing number of people who hear the Word of God preached by 144,000 Jewish followers of Jesus (Revelation 7:1–8); by 2 witnesses at the Wailing Wall (Revelation 11:1–13); and by a gospel angel heralding the news of salvation by faith in Christ alone (Revelation 14:6–7). The power of the gospel of Jesus Christ is alive and thriving in this darkest of all hours!

8. The False Prophet, as a result of this supposed resurrection, erects an image, a hologram perhaps, on a wing of the rebuilt temple. He then issues an order that all people take a mark, a number upon their right hand or forehead by which total allegiance is pledged to the Antichrist as god. The number adds up to six hundred sixty-six or 666. The mark is a tattoo pledging allegiance to and worship of the antichrist (Revelation 13:16–18)!

9. The final 1,260 days is marked with unparalleled horror as God continues to pour out 21 successive judgments on a world that hates Him and His righteousness. Famine, pestilence, ecological and geological upheavals, as well as excruciatingly painful bodily effects and death mark these judgments. However, there is also a wish to die by many, but that wish is denied!

An Amazing Prophecy

The timing of the famed "Gog/Magog War" is in dispute among prophecy students, but its surety is not in question.

> Son of man, set thy face against Gog, the land of Magog, the chief prince of Meshech and Tubal, and prophesy against him,
> And say, Thus saith the Lord GOD; Behold, I am against thee, O Gog, the chief prince of Meshech and Tubal:
> And I will turn thee back, and put hooks into thy jaws, and I will bring thee forth, and all thine army, horses and horsemen, all of them clothed with all sorts of armour, even a great company with bucklers and shields, all of them handling swords:

Persia, Ethiopia, and Libya with them; all of them with shield and helmet:

Gomer, and all his bands; the house of Togarmah of the north quarters, and all his bands: and many people with thee.

Be thou prepared, and prepare for thyself, thou, and all thy company that are assembled unto thee, and be thou a guard unto them.

After many days thou shalt be visited: in the latter years thou shalt come into the land that is brought back from the sword, and is gathered out of many people, against the mountains of Israel, which have been always waste: but it is brought forth out of the nations, and they shall dwell safely all of them.

Thou shalt ascend and come like a storm, thou shalt be like a cloud to cover the land, thou, and all thy bands, and many people with thee. (Ezekiel 38:2–9)

In Ezekiel 38–39, we read of a remarkable situation in which a northern leader suddenly decides to invade Israel. In this space, we do not want to speculate too much on the timing (other than to affirm that this great battle occurs in the last days), but we want to note something incredible: God destroys Gog's coalition army in an instant. Let's take a look at how this can happen.

Anyone who has visited Israel has seen the mountain range that runs north-south through the middle of the country. This is the exact spot where God will deal with Gog's army.

You see, on the eastern slope of the mountains of Israel, there is a steep, 3,000-foot ascent. But on the other side, the western slopes that lead to Israel's agricultural and industrial heartland, it is a gentle, 2,000-foot descent. In other words, once a giant coalition army manages to stand on the peak of the mountains, it can look west to destroy Israel with ease.

It is at that very moment that God will destroy five/sixths of Gog's army, leaving a remnant as a witness.

That soon-fulfillment is rooted in geographical and geopolitical realities right now as Russia and her Islamic and European allies lick their chops and covet what Israel owns, including vast oil and gas fields in Galilee and off the coast.

10. The 2,520th day after the signing of the Peace agreement arrives. On this day the Lord of lords, the King of kings, the Creator, sustainer, and deliverer returns to earth to take back what rightly belongs to Him. This is not the baby Jesus. This is the Warrior Judge! This is not the mild-mannered Nazarene healer the world crowned with a Cross. This is the sovereign of the universe crowned with the praises of His bride, the Church! Revelation 19:11–21 records it this way:

> And I saw heaven opened, and behold a white horse; and he that sat upon him was called Faithful and True, and in righteousness he doth judge and make war.
>
> His eyes were as a flame of fire, and on his head were many crowns; and he had a name written, that no man knew, but he himself.
>
> And he was clothed with a vesture dipped in blood: and his name is called The Word of God.
>
> And the armies which were in heaven followed him upon white horses, clothed in fine linen, white and clean.

And out of his mouth goeth a sharp sword, that with it he should smite the nations: and he shall rule them with a rod of iron: and he treadeth the winepress of the fierceness and wrath of Almighty God.

And he hath on his vesture and on his thigh a name written, KING OF KINGS, AND LORD OF LORDS.

And I saw an angel standing in the sun; and he cried with a loud voice, saying to all the fowls that fly in the midst of heaven, Come and gather yourselves together unto the supper of the great God;

That ye may eat the flesh of kings, and the flesh of captains, and the flesh of mighty men, and the flesh of horses, and of them that sit on them, and the flesh of all men, both free and bond, both small and great.

And I saw the beast, and the kings of the earth, and their armies, gathered together to make war against him that sat on the horse, and against his army.

And the beast was taken, and with him the false prophet that wrought miracles before him, with which he deceived them that had received the mark of the beast, and them that worshipped his image. These both were cast alive into a lake of fire burning with brimstone.

And the remnant were slain with the sword of him that sat upon the horse, which sword proceeded out of his mouth: and all the fowls were filled with their flesh.

That's it. The King wins! Satan loses! The False Prophet is finished! Jesus is Lord of all and over all! No planes, no bombs or missiles, no nukes, just a Word from the incarnate Word of God! Every knee shall bow and every tongue shall confess that Jesus Christ is the Lord to the glory of God the Father. But what happens to the Antichrist and all who took his mark of worship? What happens to the False Prophet? What happens to Satan? Stay tuned!

Chapter 9

The Millennial Kingdom

The armies of heaven, that is the redeemed Church of Christ, returned with their Warrior Husband and now have a front-row seat to a number of, shall we say, incredible events. Once again, we want to bullet these coming attractions.

1. The False Prophet along with the Antichrist is thrown alive into the burning lake of fire (Revelation 19:19–20).

2. Satan is bound and cast into the bottomless pit known as the abyss for the entire 1,000-year reign (Revelation 20:1–3).

3. God separates those who come to faith in Him during the seven years from those who took the mark. This is called the Sheep and Goats judgment or the Judgment of the Nations. Matthew 25:31–46 records this event as God sends those on his left, the lost to hell. Those on the right, the innumerable multitude of Revelation 7:9–11 who refused the mark, continue onto the renovated earth for 1,000 years of peace upon the earth known as the Millennium (Revelation 20:1–4).

4. Those who refused the tattoo, the mark of the beast, martyred because of their faith are now resurrected in order

that they might experience the renovated earth under the righteous reign of Jesus.

5. And he shall judge among the nations, and shall rebuke many people: and they shall beat their swords into plowshares, and their spears into pruninghooks: nation shall not lift up sword against nation, neither shall they learn war any more (Isaiah 2:4).

6. The surviving Jews will look upon Him whom they pierced and be saved by recognizing and receiving Jesus as Messiah (Zechariah 12:10; Romans 11:26). Further, they will occupy and control all the land granted to them by God in the Abrahamic covenant of Genesis 15.

7. God's created world will dwell in perfect harmony. "The wolf also shall dwell with the lamb, and the leopard shall lie down with the kid; and the calf and the young lion and the fatling together; and a little child shall lead them. And the cow and the bear shall feed; their young ones shall lie down together: and the lion shall eat straw like the ox. And the sucking child shall play on the hole of the asp, and the weaned child shall put his hand on the cockatrice' den. They shall not hurt nor destroy in all my holy mountain: for the earth shall be full of the knowledge of the LORD, as the waters cover the sea" (Isaiah 11:6–9).

8. Isaiah further writes in chapter 65:16–25. "That he who blesseth himself in the earth shall bless himself in the God of truth; and he that sweareth in the earth shall swear by the God of truth; because the former troubles are forgotten, and because they are hid from mine eyes. For, behold, I create new heavens and a new earth: and the former shall not be remembered, nor come into mind. But be ye glad and rejoice for ever in that which I create: for, behold, I create Jerusalem a rejoicing, and

her people a joy. And I will rejoice in Jerusalem, and joy in my people: and the voice of weeping shall be no more heard in her, nor the voice of crying. There shall be no more thence an infant of days, nor an old man that hath not filled his days: for the child shall die an hundred years old; but the sinner being an hundred years old shall be accursed. And they shall build houses, and inhabit them; and they shall plant vineyards, and eat the fruit of them. They shall not build, and another inhabit; they shall not plant, and another eat: for as the days of a tree are the days of my people, and mine elect shall long enjoy the work of their hands. They shall not labour in vain, nor bring forth for trouble; for they are the seed of the blessed of the LORD, and their offspring with them. And it shall come to pass, that before they call, I will answer; and while they are yet speaking, I will hear. The wolf and the lamb shall feed together, and the lion shall eat straw like the bullock: and dust shall be the serpent's meat. They shall not hurt nor destroy in all my holy mountain, saith the LORD."

Peace, real peace, true peace — and yet there will still be sin deep in the heart of some. When the Millennium begins it will be comprised of two kinds of beings. First and foremost will be the redeemed of Christ, the Bride, the raptured Church that was caught up to the Father's house and gloriously changed, receiving a body like Christ. Imagine not being bound by time or space. Imagine not gaining weight while eating the delicacies of heaven. This is the redeemed!

The second kind of millennial inhabitants will be those who gave their lives to Christ, rejected the Mark/tattoo and managed to survive the Tribulation years. They will enter the reign of peace in their natural, physical, unredeemed bodies. As such they will continue to procreate and the population will explode. Once again people will live extended lives due to the lack of ultraviolet rays, lack of sickness and disease as a result of foods filled with chemicals, and greed-driven businesses putting money over morals. Isaiah reminds us that one who dies at 100 years of age will be looked upon as a mere child!

However, each and every birth is one born with the same fallen sin nature we experience today. The battle will continue as to who will be Lord of their lives? You would certainly think that each and every one would choose Jesus and His love and yet . . . they don't.

Some of the most shocking words found in the Word of God are these:

> And when the thousand years are expired, Satan shall be loosed out of his prison,
>
> And shall go out to deceive the nations which are in the four quarters of the earth, Gog, and Magog, to gather them together to battle: the number of whom is as the sand of the sea.
>
> And they went up on the breadth of the earth, and compassed the camp of the saints about, and the beloved city: and fire came down from God out of heaven, and devoured them.
>
> And the devil that deceived them was cast into the lake of fire and brimstone, where the beast and the false prophet are, and shall be tormented day and night for ever and ever (Revelation 20:7–10).

How can it be? Why would anyone follow the unleashed Satan straight into hell for all eternity and yet the number will be "as the sand upon the seashore"! Staggering! Shocking!

Why would God allow it? Could it be that He does so in order to refute the humanistic idea that if you place a person in a good and nurturing environment they will choose to do what is right and good. They do not! It isn't the economy, it isn't the environment, it's the heart!

Chapter 10

Glory

And if we are Christians, let us not hesitate to adopt as true to fact the account of miracles and the prediction of future events, inasmuch as the whole Christian system is itself a miracle from the creation to the constitution of the new heavens and the new earth wherein dwelleth righteousness.[1] — Robert Dick Wilson

Each Christmas, part of the joy of the season is to sing the great hymns in church. Most of us of a certain age remember these services fondly, even somewhat imagining them in our memories as something akin to a Norman Rockwell painting.

It would be hard to pick a number one favorite Christmas hymn — so many come to mind — but "Joy to the World" certainly ranks right up there.

> Joy to the world! The Lord is come
> Let earth receive her King!
> Let every heart prepare Him room
>
> And heaven and nature sing
> And heaven and nature sing
> And heaven, and heaven and nature sing

---

1. Robert Dick Wilson, "The Rule of Faith and Life," *The Princeton Theological Review*, vol. 26, no. 3, July 1928, p. 430.

Joy to the world! the Savior reigns
Let men their songs employ
While fields and floods
Rocks, hills and plains
Repeat the sounding joy
Repeat the sounding joy
Repeat, repeat the sounding joy

No more let sins and sorrows grow
Nor thorns infest the ground
He comes to make
His blessings flow
Far as the curse is found
Far as the curse is found
Far as, far as the curse is found

He rules the world with truth and grace
And makes the nations prove
The glories of His righteousness
And wonders of His love
And wonders of His love
And wonders and wonders of His love.[2]

Did you notice the lyrics? In one of the great ironies, we think that if you would ask, the vast majority of people would think the song speaks of the birth of Jesus — the real Christmas story.

It does not.

"Joy to the World," written by Isaac Watts in 1719, and based on Psalm 98, looks ahead to the coming Redeemer, Jesus Christ.

It is about His Second Coming!

Notice the fourth and fifth stanzas, which speak of the ushering in of righteousness and joy in a world marred by sin. The song describes a re-created world, celebrating God's faithfulness to the nation of Israel, which brings salvation to the world. In that day all true Christ followers. whether they be Jew or Arab,

---

2. http://www.metrolyrics.com/joy-to-the-world-lyrics-christmas-carols.html.

white man or black man, and everyone in between, will be reconciled to their God and to each other.

It is a day lovers of Yeshua the Messiah, Jesus Christ the Lord, should anticipate with great joy. Let's look at Psalm 98:

O sing unto the LORD a new song; for he hath done marvellous things: his right hand, and his holy arm, hath gotten him the victory.

The LORD hath made known his salvation: his righteousness hath he openly shewed in the sight of the heathen.

He hath remembered his mercy and his truth toward the house of Israel: all the ends of the earth have seen the salvation of our God.

Make a joyful noise unto the LORD, all the earth: make a loud noise, and rejoice, and sing praise.

Sing unto the LORD with the harp; with the harp, and the voice of a psalm.

With trumpets and sound of cornet make a joyful noise before the LORD, the King.

Let the sea roar, and the fulness thereof; the world, and they that dwell therein.

Let the floods clap their hands: let the hills be joyful together

Before the LORD; for he cometh to judge the earth: with righteousness shall he judge the world, and the people with equity.

Isn't that incredible? When the Lord ushers in His glory, both mankind and nature itself will sing with joy. It should be noted, too, that like thousands of other passages in the Bible, these promises from God are not some pie-in-the-sky, dreamy, otherworldly stuff that has no practical value for us. On the contrary, precisely *because* we see the astonishing fulfillment of predictive prophecy all through the Bible — particularly where it relates to Israel — we can know for sure that God is bringing glory to His creation.

Think of it: no more pain, no more sorrow, no more mental, physical, or emotional anguish. In Isaiah 65:18–25, we read about this plan of God, in which He moves from the judgment phase of His plan, to a new world, one free of pain and suffering:

> But be ye glad and rejoice for ever in that which I create: for, behold, I create Jerusalem a rejoicing, and her people a joy.
>
> And I will rejoice in Jerusalem, and joy in my people: and the voice of weeping shall be no more heard in her, nor the voice of crying.
>
> There shall be no more thence an infant of days, nor an old man that hath not filled his days: for the child shall die an hundred years old; but the sinner being an hundred years old shall be accursed.
>
> And they shall build houses, and inhabit them; and they shall plant vineyards, and eat the fruit of them.
>
> They shall not build, and another inhabit; they shall not plant, and another eat: for as the days of a tree are the days of my people, and mine elect shall long enjoy the work of their hands.
>
> They shall not labour in vain, nor bring forth for trouble; for they are the seed of the blessed of the LORD, and their offspring with them.
>
> And it shall come to pass, that before they call, I will answer; and while they are yet speaking, I will hear.
>
> The wolf and the lamb shall feed together, and the lion shall eat straw like the bullock: and dust shall be the serpent's meat. They shall not hurt nor destroy in all my holy mountain, saith the LORD.

We see then that this world, once described by Tennyson as "red in tooth and claw,"[3] in other words a savage world of death, will one day be redeemed forevermore.

---

3. Alfred Lord Tennyson, "In Memoriam A.H.H.," 1849.

If you the reader have placed your trust in Jesus Christ, you have assurance that God's Word is sure. Because the Creator God has proven Himself time after time after time, can we not logically see that He will fulfill all He has promised, most importantly the great end-times promises of renewal and peace?

The evidence that God keeps His promises is overwhelming, heavy, compelling. Yet we know that most people are skeptical.

Bertrand Russell was one of those people. He is one of, if not the most famous atheists known to man in recent years. The *New Yorker* magazine reported in 1963 concerning a conversation that took place at Russell's 90th birthday gathering. It seems a lady from London sat next to him and asked him, "What will you do Bertie, if it turns out you were wrong?" she asked. "I mean, what if — uh — when the time comes, you should meet Him? What will you say?" Russell was delighted with the question. His bright, birdlike eyes grew even brighter as he contemplated this possible future dialogue, and then he pointed a finger upward and cried, "Why, I should say, 'God, you gave us insufficient evidence.'"

That is an amazing response from a man considered to be a leading intellectual light. For the root issue of such a response centers on the fact that people are arrogant and stubborn. No more arrogant and stubborn than when they come up against the parameters set up by the Creator. The Creator has given not just ample evidence for His existence, but overwhelming evidence.

This matters in the real world in which we live. These are issues that matter to the individual. Each of us lives a full life, varied as they are. But in the end, God has brought about the ultimate miracle: each person in history has an opportunity to know and be reconciled to his or her Creator.

There is an extraordinary prophecy recorded in Revelation 21:1: "And I saw a new heaven and a new earth: for the first heaven and the first earth were passed away; and there was no more sea."

The scholar Henry M. Morris had this to say about the passage:

> Note that Christ's prophecy, made long ago (Matthew 24:35), will finally be fulfilled, the only entity surviving from that previous world being the eternal Word of God (Psalm 119:160).[4]

According to Dr. John Walvoord there are 1,000 prophecies in Scripture, of which 500 have already been fulfilled, how can we not look ahead with great anticipation to the fulfillment of this one?

If we are indeed on the very edge of the end of human history, what are some evidences we can cite, evidences that presumably men like Bertrand Russell demanded?

Well, let's note some clues that we are living in the very end of history, some of them repeated from previous chapters. Here, we primarily will focus on the one great evidence: the international obsession with the tiny nation of Israel. The Jewish state is not so slowly being squeezed in the court of public opinion. We have only to look at the latest of many Palestinian terror waves in Israel; stabbings, shootings, even vehicles being used as weapons.

Through that latest instance of hostility toward the Jewish people, we see the international community condemning whom? The Palestinians? No, it is the same as it has been since 1948. Israel! Surely this kind of irrational behavior is found in the previously discussed spiritual hatred of Jews (see Genesis 3:15).

Let us then look at a list of facts pointing to Israel as the focal point of the end of history.

Israeli Sovereignty over Jerusalem

With Zechariah 10–14 as the backdrop for this section, we can note several evidences that the international community ("the nations" according to Scripture) absolutely loathes Israel.

---

4. Henry M. Morris, *The Henry Morris Study Bible* (Green Forest, AR: Master Books, 2012), p. 2039, commentary note for Revelation 21:1.

In the spring of 1997, bulldozers worked day and night to create the space needed for a new community in East Jerusalem, Har Homa.

Natural growth in Jewish communities seems to bother the world. The world is not bothered by natural growth in Paris or Lisbon or Milwaukee or Beijing. The international community is greatly bothered by Jewish births, which leads to the need for more housing. It was reported on March 13, 1997, that the General Assembly of the United Nations voted to censure Israel for building in Har Homa.

> While the United States and Israel were the only two countries to vote against the resolution condemning the new Jewish neighborhood, 130 countries voted in favor of it. Micronesia and the Marshall Islands abstained. Fifty-one members of the 185-nation Assembly did not take part in the vote.[5]

In the view of the writers, the number one evidence that we are in the last of the last days, and thus on the cusp of God's final end-times plans and the ushering in of glory, is the international stranglehold tightening on the state of Israel.

Remember, Zechariah predicted through the inspiration of the Lord that Jerusalem itself would become a burdensome stone for the nations of the world. In other words, there would be a reason, a trigger, for their obsession. That reason is the sovereignty of Israel over the entire city since June 1967.

Ten years after the Oslo Accords, even religious leaders began to notice the status of Jerusalem:

> The peace of the world depends directly on the future of Jerusalem, the visiting Archbishop of Canterbury has told a meeting of Christians in the Middle East. In an open letter, Dr. Rowan Williams said there was "small

---

5. Paul Lewis, "Israel's Plan For Jerusalem Is Condemned By Assembly," The New York Times, March 14, 1997, p. A6.

hope of lasting reconciliation in the wider world" without "peace and justice for all the peoples of the Holy Land."[6]

Incredibly, even the archbishop, certainly no Zionist, recognized the intensifying pressure on Israel with regard to the status of the Holy City:

> "Even ten years ago, few people would have thought the day would come when the peace of the world would depend so directly on the peace of Jerusalem," the Archbishop concluded.[7]

Wow. Let us look again at the marvelously detailed prophecy from Zechariah regarding Jerusalem in the last days:

> For I will gather all nations against Jerusalem to battle; and the city shall be taken, and the houses rifled, and the women ravished; and half of the city shall go forth into captivity, and the residue of the people shall not be cut off from the city (Zechariah 14:2).

All the nations. This scenario has, to this point, never happened in all of history.

At the end of the Clinton presidency, when the White House was working feverishly to broker a final peace deal between the terrorist Arafat (grandson of Haj Amin Al-Husseini, Grand Mufti of Jerusalem, who was a counselor to Hitler concerning the annihilation of the Jews) and the Israelis, the Dalai Lama visited Jerusalem and called for peace. Sadly, he showed no biblical understanding of the world's paramount hotspot:

> Human beings should consider other human beings as fellow brothers and sisters. The differences of ideology, systems and nationality are secondary.[8]

---

6. ICEJ [International Christian Embassy Jerusalem] News Service From Jerusalem, April 15, 2003.
7. Ibid.
8. The Associated Press, "Dalai Lama Calls for Peace in Jerusalem," June 15, 1999.

In an extraordinary acknowledgment that all the enormous diplomatic efforts down through the decades have utterly failed, we saw in the last days of the Clinton presidency that perhaps the world should recognize the only true, possible solution to the fight over Jerusalem:

> Israelis and Palestinians who have spent months wrangling over which side should control Jerusalem's holy sites are turning their attention to an idea first floated at Camp David: Put God in charge.
>
> The proposal to declare God the sovereign over Jerusalem shrines that are holy to both Muslims and Jews is still tentative, but it has the potential to help defuse the most emotional dispute in the Mideast peace talks.
>
> It has won the guarded endorsement of Jerusalem's hawkish Israeli mayor and a top Palestinian official — marking the first time the two sides have found any common ground on how to share the city.[9]

The Echo of Empires

Following closely in the realm of evidences that we are on the very edge of glory is the acknowledgment of both Jews and Christians that Israel's very rebirth is a monumental miracle.

Isi Leibler, once a leading Zionist in the Diaspora (from his business perch in Australia), wrote in 2003 about the gargantuan fulfillment of Israel's return:

> Let us tell the defeatists and pessimists to focus on all the empires and civilizations that preceded us and sought to destroy us. They are no longer. Yet we are here in our ancestral homeland.
>
> To have risen like a phoenix from the ashes of the Holocaust and resurrected statehood after an interval

---

9. The Associated Press, "God's Control Posed as Jerusalem Solution," August 31, 2000.

of 20 centuries is surely no less of a miracle than the Exodus.[10]

Gary Anderson, a professor of history at Notre Dame, is a rare academic who gives a nod to the miraculous:

> What God has given He can also take away, and on at least two occasions — the destruction of Jerusalem in 586 B.C. and A.D. 70 — Israel has been driven into exile. And yet, unlike the Hittites, the people of Israel have endured. Wherever they are driven they remain unassimilated.
>
> The miraculous appearance of the Israeli state just after the darkest moment in Jewish history is hard to interpret outside of a theological framework.[11]

And then Anderson puts a fine point on it:

> The fact that Israel has lasted two millennia without a homeland or any sort of native rule is miraculous.[12]

The Rise of the "Christian Palestinianists"

Running parallel to the geopolitical world turning on Israel is the strange and disconcerting switch in allegiance by American Christian leadership where Israel is concerned.

Interestingly, evangelical leaders in Asia and Africa often clearly see the importance of Israel and the Jews. Their counterparts in American ministry seem clueless about the specialness of the Jews. We feel strongly that the melding of political and religious dislikes of Israel is a strong indicator that we are in the very last of the last days.

David Parsons has been a key contributor to the International Christian Embassy in Jerusalem for a long time. He is the one of the first to observe the tendency of Palestinian leaders to

---

10. "Counting Israel's Blessings," *The Jerusalem Post*, April 15, 2003.
11. Gary A. Anderson, "How to Think About Zionism," *First Things*, April 2005, p. 30–36.
12. Ibid.

enlist the help of Palestinian Christians in marginalizing Israel. He then notes the spillover effect in America:

> Meanwhile, though most Evangelical Christians have long tended to hold a favorable view of Israel for biblical and moral reasons, some Evangelicals began gravitating towards a pro-Palestinian stand. Many were impacted by the tales of suffering they heard and read from local Arab Christians, chief among them being Father Elias Chacour.[13]

Since Chacour, author of *Blood Brothers*, other Palestinian Christian leaders have emerged to partner with their friends in America. Sami Awad of the Holy Land Trust is perhaps the key person bringing the so-called Palestinian Narrative — which undermines Israel's legitimacy — into American churches.

Awad has partnered with friends like Lynne Hybels (the wife of Bill Hybels, co-founders of the Willow Creek Association), Mae Cannon of World Vision, and young pastors like Jonathan Martin to defame Israel in church presentations.

The fulfillment of Zechariah 10–14 was never going to come about solely through the efforts of geopolitics. It would have to be ushered in by the coming of the New World Order overall, which includes a one-world religion.

We have not seen the end of this goal of undermining Israel in American churches, and we grieve over it. In a broader sense, though, it is part of the fulfillment of Zechariah that will see a final battle over the status of Jerusalem. This is but another sign that we are in the very last of the last days.

Dear reader, the grand stage of history is being set for the final act. When you boil it down, the various eras fade away and each of us stands in the spotlight.

Where are you going after you die? If you live to see the upheaval that is coming to civilization, what will happen to you?

---

13. David Parsons, "Swords into Ploughshares: Christian Zionism and the Battle of Armageddon," International Christian Embassy Jerusalem, p. 11.

Through it all, we see the continuity of Israel and its place in history. As Claude Duvernoy has written:

> After Titus and his legions of destruction, after the edicts of contempt and hate of a "Christian" empire, after the autos-da-fe and the pogroms, after Auschwitz and the miraculous rebirth in 1948 — is there a better and clearer manifestation of the grace of God than this Zionist epic which is still in progress?[14]

Through the story of Israel, we track our own story. That story is coming to a close.

Final Thoughts

The Jewish people have experienced pain, suffering, and death through the centuries, and yet terrible dark days lie ahead. Zechariah 13:8 tells us:

> And it shall come to pass, that in all the land, saith the LORD, two parts [thirds] therein shall be cut off and die; but the third shall be left therein.

Imagine! Two-thirds of all the Jewish people living in Israel, close to 7 million today, will die. Over 4 million of these precious ones will be killed. Another Holocaust is on its way.

Will you look at the miracle that is Israel and realize there truly is a God who is at work and His world clock is ticking?

Would you dare to challenge the facts? God loves the Jew. He also loves the Gentile. In fact, God so loved the world that He gave. . . .

Gave what, you ask? No, gave who? Gave the Lord Jesus Christ to do for each of us what we could never do for ourselves. What did He do for me, you ask? He paid the penalty for your sin and mine.

---

14. Claude Duvernoy, *Controversy of Zion* (Green Forest, AR: New Leaf Press, 1987), p. 222.

Without the shedding of blood there is no remission of sin (Hebrews 9:22).

The sinless God-man willingly took upon Himself all our sin: past, present, and future (Psalm 103:12). He gave His sinless life in exchange for our sinful life. It's hard to believe, but it is true. He loves us that much.

Everyone in this hard, cruel world wants and desperately needs love, forgiveness, and acceptance. Many search a lifetime and yet never come to understand that what their hearts long for is found in Jesus! He gives love, joy, peace, forgiveness, and acceptance. Best of all, it's free for the asking.

> For the wages of sin is death; but the gift of God is eternal life through Jesus Christ our Lord (Romans 6:23).

> And it shall come to pass, that whosoever shall call on the name of the Lord shall be saved (Acts 2:21).

Have you? Will you?

The very fact that God is and will make good on His promises to the Jew is proof positive He will keep each and every promise He has made to all who choose to follow Him.

Join me; let's walk together hand in hand with Jesus into the New Jerusalem for all of eternity.

The Last Word

Because God is so precise in what He does, it makes sense that He would choose such a big historical stage on which to bring back the Jews. Two thousand years of exile gave way to statehood in 1948 — over and over again in Scripture, He had promised this.

Think about that very carefully.

The Jewish community worldwide has been harassed and hunted for 4,000 years. They have been fearful, uncertain, unhealthy, poverty stricken, their jobs have been taken away, their children have been wayward . . . they've even wondered where God is in all of it.

Sound familiar?

We would ask that after reading this book you meditate on the miraculous story of the nation of Israel — always on the edge of extinction, yet upheld by the strong hand of God. And now, finally, after everyone had written them off, they are back forevermore.

Your life is like that, if you live long enough on this planet. You might be suffering from bad health, a lost career, persecution, character assassination, or what have you. You might be going through your own personal exile. It hurts.

But think of it this way: if God can manage to return His little band of Chosen People to their ancient land where they now thrive — and He brought all this about with precision and perfection that cannot be explained away — then He is certainly ready, willing, and able to do the same for you. No question.

The Jews should have been gone from the earth a long time ago, as the Hittites and Scythians are. They should have been, but they aren't. They live and breathe and find joy and purpose in the Land of Israel, today, right now. What that means for you is that you too can rise from the ashes, anew and full of life.

When you let all that sink in, you'll be able to write your own story. We invite you to do that and marvel at the mercies of the Lord. Just as the Jews were restored, so too does the Lord want to restore you, so that you have your own story:

*The Miracle of*_____

I will repay you for the years the locusts have eaten (Joel 2:25).

Appendix I

Prophecies Fulfilled at the First Coming of Christ

There are over 300 prophecies in the Old Testament about the first coming of Christ, but many of these are repetitious. When the repetitious ones are deleted, we are still left with at least 108 specifically different prophecies — all of which were fulfilled in the birth, life, death, and Resurrection of Christ.

The fulfillment of so many prophecies in the life of one person is overwhelming proof that Jesus is the Messiah of God. The odds of so many prophecies being fulfilled coincidentally in the life of any person are far beyond the realm of probability. Fulfilled prophecy is thus one of the most substantial proofs that Jesus was who He said He was — namely, the anointed Son of God (Mark 14:62–63).

Old Testament Reference	Prophecy	New Testament Fulfillment
A. The Messiah's Lineage		
Gen. 9:26	1) From the Shemite Branch of Humanity	Luke 3:36
Gen. 12:3	2) Through Abraham	Matt. 1:1
Gen. 17:21	3) Through Abraham's son, Isaac	Luke 3:34
Gen. 28:14	4) Through Isaac's son, Jacob	Luke 3:34

Gen. 49:8	5) Through the tribe of Judah	Luke 3:33–34
Isa. 11:1	6) Through the family of Jesse	Luke 3:32
Jer. 23:5	7) Through the house of David	Luke 3:31–32

B. The Messiah's Birth and Childhood

Gen. 49:10	1) Timing of birth. According to the Talmud, in about 7 A.D. the Romans removed the power of the Sanhedrin Council in Judah to pronounce the death penalty — thus the scepter (power) passed from Judah. Jesus had been born in 4 B.C. during the reign of Herod (Mark 2:1), so "Shiloh" (a Messianic title) had come shortly before the sceptre departed — just as prophesied. Also, once the Jews were expelled from the land by the Romans, all semblance of national autonomy under Judah was gone.	
Mic. 5:2	2) Place of birth	Matt. 2:1
Isa. 9:6	3) Born in the flesh	Luke 2:11
Isa. 7:14	4) Born of a virgin	Luke 1:34–35
Isa. 7:14	5) Divine name	Matt. 1:21
Ps. 72:10–11	6) Presented with gifts at birth	Matt. 2:1–12
Jer. 31:15	7) Infants massacred	Matt. 2:16
Hos. 11:1	8) Sojourn in Egypt	Matt. 2:14–15
Isa. 11:1; 53:3*	9) Reside in Nazareth	Matt. 2:23
Isa. 53:2	10) Grow up in obscurity and poverty	Mark 6:3
Isa. 11:1	11) Spirit-filled and anointed from birth	Luke 2:46–47

*Matthew's reference is uncertain. Some believe it is derived from Isaiah 11:1 where the Messiah is referred to as a "neser" — that is, a "branch" of Jesse.

C. The Messiah's Life and Ministry

Isa. 40:3	1) Preceded by a prophet preparing His way	Matt. 3:1–3
Isa. 42:1	2) Receive a special anointing by the Holy Spirit	Luke 3:22
Gen. 3:15	3) Do battle with Satan	Matt. 4:1
Ps. 91:11	4) Receive the ministry of angels	Matt. 4:11
Isa. 9:1	5) Ministry centered in Galilee	Matt. 4:13
Isa. 42:2	6) Unpretentious ministry	John 6:15
Isa. 53:2	7) Power of ministry not based on personal appearance	Matt. 7:28–29
Ps. 40:9	8) Preacher	Matt. 4:17
Ps. 78:2	9) Teacher in parables	Matt. 13:34–35
Deut. 18:15,18	10) Prophet	Matt. 21:11
Isa. 33:22	11) Judge	John 5:30
Isa. 11:2	12) Miracle worker	John 3:2
Ps. 109:4	13) Man of prayer	Luke 18:1
Ps. 22:9–10	14) Man whose reliance and trust is in God	John 5:19

Ps. 40:8	15) Man of obedience	John 4:34
Isa. 11:2	16) Man of knowledge, wisdom, and understanding	Matt. 13:54
Isa. 11:2	17) Man of counsel	John 3:1–4
Zech. 9:9	18) Humble in spirit	Phil. 2:8
Ps. 145:8	19) Patient	1 Tim. 1:16
Ps. 103:17	20) Loving and merciful	John 15:13
Ps. 69:9	21) Zeal for God's house in Jerusalem	John 2:14–16
Isa. 61:1–2	22) Proclaim a Jubilee	Luke 4:17–21
Isa. 61:1	23) Preach the gospel to the poor	Matt. 11:4–5
Isa. 61:1	24) Comfort the brokenhearted	Matt. 11:28
Isa. 61:1	25) Proclaim liberty to captives	Luke 4:18
Isa. 42:3	26) Minister to broken lives	Luke 5:30–31
Isa. 53:5	27) Heal the sick	Matt. 8:16–17
Isa. 35:5–6	28) Heal those with special afflictions	Matt. 11:4–5
Ps. 69:4	29) Hated without cause	John 15:24–25
Ps. 69:7–8	30) Despised and rejected by His own people, the Jews	John 1:11
Isa. 29:13	31) Rejected by the Jews due to exaltation of tradition	Mark 7:6–8
Ps. 8:2	32) Praised by babes and infants	Matt. 21:15–16
Isa. 49:6	33) Offered to the Gentiles	John 1:12
Hos. 2:23	34) Accepted by the Gentiles	Acts 28:28

D. The Messiah's Nature

Mic. 5:2	1) Eternal	John 1:1
Isa. 9:6	2) Divine	John 10:30
Ps. 8:5	3) Human	John 1:14
Ps. 2:7	4) Son of God	Matt. 3:17
Dan. 7:13	5) Son of Man	Matt. 8:20
Ps. 2:2	6) Christ, the Anointed One	Luke 2:10–11
Ps. 110:1	7) Lord	John 13:13
Isa. 11:2–3	8) God centered	John 17:4
Isa. 5:16	9) Holy	Heb. 7:26
Isa. 53:11	10) Righteous	Acts 7:52
Ps. 89:1–2	11) Faithful and true witness	Rev. 3:14
Isa. 42:1	12) Servant of God	Phil. 2:6–7
Ps. 23:1	13) Loving shepherd	John 10:11
Isa. 53:7	14) Sacrificial lamb	John 1:29
Isa. 53:4–6	15) Sin bearer	1 Pet. 2:24
Isa. 53:10	16) Guilt offering	Heb. 9:13–14
Isa. 42:6	17) Embodiment of God's Redemptive Covenant	Acts 13:47

E. The Messiah's Death

Dan. 9:25–26 1) Timing of death. The prophecy states that the Messiah will die 69 weeks of years (483 yrs.) after the edict is issued to rebuild Jerusalem. The edict was issued by Artaxerxes in 445 B.C., and 483 lunar years later Jesus was crucified in Jerusalem.

Zech. 9:9	2) Triumphal entry into Jerusalem	John 12:12–15
Isa. 53:3, 11	3) Experience profound grief and agony	Matt. 26:37–38
Ps. 41:9	4) Betrayal by a friend who would eat with Him	Matt. 26:20–21
Zech. 11:12	5) Betrayal for 30 pieces of silver	Matt. 26:14–15
Zech. 11:13	6) Disposition of the betrayal money	Matt. 27:3, 5–7
Zech. 13:7	7) Forsaken by His disciples	Matt. 26:55–56
Ps. 35:11–12	8) Accused by false witnesses	Matt. 26:59
Is. 53:7	9) Silent before His accusers	Matt. 27:14
Isa. 50:6	10) Spat upon	Matt. 26:67
Mic. 5:1	11) Stricken	Matt. 26:67
Isa. 50:6	12) Scourged	Matt. 27:26
Isa. 52:14	13) Face beaten to a pulp	Matt. 27:30
Isa. 50:6	14) Beard plucked. There is no specific recorded fulfillment of this prophecy, but it was likely one of the tortures inflicted upon Jesus by the soldiers.	
Isa. 50:6	15) Humiliated	Mark 15:17-19
Ps. 22:15	16) Physical exhaustion	Luke 23:26
Ps. 22:16	17) Crucified	Luke 23:33
Isa. 53:12	18) Identified with sinners	Mark 15:27
Ps. 22:6–8	19) Object of scorn and ridicule	Luke 23:35–39
Ps. 22:15	20) Experienced thirst	John 19:28
Ps. 69:21	21) Given vinegar to drink	Matt. 27:48
Ps. 38:11	22) Friends stand far away	Luke 23:49
Ps. 22:17	23) Stared at	Luke 23:35
Ps. 22:18	24) Clothing divided among persecutors	John 19:23
Ps. 22:18	25) Lots cast for robe	John 19:23–24
Amos 8:9	26) Darkness at noon	Matt. 27:45
Ps. 22:1	27) A cry of disorientation due to separation from God	Matt. 27:46
Ps. 109:4	28) Pray for persecutors	Luke 23:34
Ps. 22:31*	29) Cry of victory	John 19:30
Ps. 31:5	30) Voluntary release of spirit	Luke 23:46
Ps. 34:20	31) No bones broken	John 19:32–33
Zech. 12:10	32) Pierced in the side	John 19:34
Ps. 22:14**	33) Death by a broken heart	John 19:34
Isa. 53:9	34) Buried in a rich man's grave	Matt. 27:57–60

*The phrase, "He hath done this," literally means, "He has finished it."
**The separation of the blood and water is a sign of a ruptured heart.

F. The Messiah's Resurrection and Ascension

Ps. 16:10	1) Resurrection	Mark 16:6
Ps. 68:18	2) Ascension	Acts 1:9
Ps. 110:1	3) Exaltation at the right hand of God	Mark 16:19
Ps. 110:4	4) Serve as a High Priest	Heb. 6:20
Ps. 2:1–2	5) Continue to be despised by the nations	1 John 5:19

This listing has been adapted, with minor changes, from *Lamplighter* (July/August 1990; vol. xi).

Appendix II

Israel's Declaration of Independence

THE DECLARATION:

ERETZ-ISRAEL (the Land of Israel) was the birthplace of the Jewish people. Here their spiritual, religious and political identity was shaped. Here they first attained to statehood, created cultural values of national and universal significance and gave to the world the eternal Book of Books.

After being forcibly exiled from their land, the people kept faith with it throughout their Dispersion and never ceased to pray and hope for their return to it and for the restoration in it of their political freedom.

Impelled by this historic and traditional attachment, Jews strove in every successive generation to re-establish themselves in their ancient homeland. In recent decades they returned in their masses. Pioneers, ma'pilim (immigrants coming to Eretz-Israel in defiance of restrictive legislation) and defenders, they made deserts bloom, revived the Hebrew language, built villages and towns, and created a thriving community controlling its own economy and culture, loving peace but knowing how to defend itself, bringing the blessings of progress to all the country's inhabitants, and aspiring towards independent nationhood.

In the year 5657 (1897), at the summons of the spiritual father of the Jewish State, Theodore Herzl, the First Zionist Congress convened and proclaimed the right of the Jewish people to national rebirth in its own country.

This right was recognized in the Balfour Declaration of the 2nd November, 1917, and re-affirmed in the Mandate of the League of Nations which, in particular, gave international sanction to the historic connection between the Jewish people and Eretz-Israel and to the right of the Jewish people to rebuild its National Home.

The catastrophe which recently befell the Jewish people — the massacre of millions of Jews in Europe — was another clear demonstration of the urgency of solving the problem of its homelessness by re-establishing in Eretz-Israel the Jewish State, which would open the gates of the homeland wide to every Jew and confer upon the Jewish people the status of a fully privileged member of the community of nations.

Survivors of the Nazi holocaust in Europe, as well as Jews from other parts of the world, continued to migrate to Eretz-Israel, undaunted by difficulties, restrictions and dangers, and never ceased to assert their right to a life of dignity, freedom and honest toil in their national homeland.

In the Second World War, the Jewish community of this country contributed its full share to the struggle of the freedom- and peace-loving nations against the forces of Nazi wickedness and, by the blood of its soldiers and its war effort, gained the right to be reckoned among the peoples who founded the United Nations.

On the 29th November, 1947, the United Nations General Assembly passed a resolution calling for the establishment of a Jewish State in Eretz-Israel; the General Assembly required the inhabitants of Eretz-Israel to take such steps as were necessary on their part for the implementation of that resolution. This recognition by the United Nations of the right of the Jewish people to establish their State is irrevocable.

This right is the natural right of the Jewish people to be masters of their own fate, like all other nations, in their own sovereign State.

ACCORDINGLY WE, MEMBERS OF THE PEOPLE'S COUNCIL, REPRESENTATIVES OF THE JEWISH COMMUNITY OF ERETZ-ISRAEL AND OF THE ZIONIST MOVEMENT, ARE HERE ASSEMBLED ON THE DAY OF THE TERMINATION OF THE BRITISH MANDATE OVER ERETZ-ISRAEL AND, BY VIRTUE OF OUR NATURAL AND HISTORIC RIGHT AND ON THE STRENGTH OF THE RESOLUTION OF THE UNITED NATIONS GENERAL ASSEMBLY, HEREBY DECLARE THE ESTABLISHMENT OF A JEWISH STATE IN ERETZ-ISRAEL, TO BE KNOWN AS THE STATE OF ISRAEL.

WE DECLARE that, with effect from the moment of the termination of the Mandate being tonight, the eve of Sabbath, the 6th Iyar, 5708 (15th May, 1948), until the establishment of the elected, regular authorities of the State in accordance with the Constitution which shall be adopted by the Elected Constituent Assembly not later than the 1st October 1948, the People's Council shall act as a Provisional Council of State, and its executive organ, the People's Administration, shall be the Provisional Government of the Jewish State, to be called "Israel."

THE STATE OF ISRAEL will be open for Jewish immigration and for the Ingathering of the Exiles; it will foster the development of the country for the benefit of all its inhabitants; it will be based on freedom, justice and peace as envisaged by the prophets of Israel; it will ensure complete equality of social and political rights to all its inhabitants irrespective of religion, race or sex; it will guarantee freedom of religion, conscience, language, education and culture; it will safeguard the Holy Places of all religions; and it will be faithful to the principles of the Charter of the United Nations.

THE STATE OF ISRAEL is prepared to cooperate with the agencies and representatives of the United Nations in implementing the resolution of the General Assembly of the 29th November, 1947, and will take steps to bring about the economic union of the whole of Eretz-Israel.

WE APPEAL to the United Nations to assist the Jewish people in the building-up of its State and to receive the State of Israel into the comity of nations.

WE APPEAL — in the very midst of the onslaught launched against us now for months — to the Arab inhabitants of the State of Israel to preserve peace and participate in the upbuilding of the State on the basis of full and equal citizenship and due representation in all its provisional and permanent institutions.

WE EXTEND our hand to all neighbouring states and their peoples in an offer of peace and good neighbourliness, and appeal to them to establish bonds of cooperation and mutual help with the sovereign Jewish people settled in its own land. The State of Israel is prepared to do its share in a common effort for the advancement of the entire Middle East.

WE APPEAL to the Jewish people throughout the Diaspora to rally round the Jews of Eretz-Israel in the tasks of immigration and upbuilding and to stand by them in the great struggle for the realization of the age-old dream — the redemption of Israel.

PLACING OUR TRUST IN THE ALMIGHTY, WE AFFIX OUR SIGNATURES TO THIS PROCLAMATION AT THIS SESSION OF THE PROVISIONAL COUNCIL OF STATE, ON THE SOIL OF THE HOMELAND, IN THE CITY OF TEL-AVIV, ON THIS SABBATH EVE, THE 5TH DAY OF IYAR, 5708 - 14TH MAY, 1948.

David Ben-Gurion

Rabbi Kalman Kahana	Sa'adia Kobashi
Aharon Zisling	Daniel Auster
Yitzhak Ben Zvi	Rachel Cohen

David Zvi Pinkas

Mordechai Bentov

Moshe Kolodny

Eliyahu Berligne

Rabbi Yitzchak Meir Levin

Eliezer Kaplan

Fritz Bernstein

Abraham Katznelson

Rabbi Wolf Gold

Meir David Loewenstein

Felix Rosenblueth

Meir Grabovsky

David Remez

Yitzchak Gruenbaum

Zvi Luria

Berl Repetur

Dr. Abraham Granovsky

Golda Myerson

Mordekhai Shattner

Nachum Nir

Ben Zion Sternberg

Eliyahu Dobkin

Zvi Segal

Bekhor Shitreet

Meir Wilner-Kovner

Rabbi Yehuda Leib Hacohen
 Fishman

Moshe Shapira

 Zerach Wahrhaftig

 Moshe Shertok

 Herzl Vardi

Fulfillment of Biblical Prophecies

One of the strong evidences of divine inspiration of the Bible (not found in other religious books of either past or present) consists of its hundreds of fulfilled prophecies. These are not vague or ambiguous (as in various occult writings) but are specific and detailed, often made hundreds or thousands of years in advance. Many are being fulfilled today, thereby indicating the probable early return of the Lord Jesus Christ.

I. The Histories of Nations

Egypt was, with Babylonia, one of the two greatest nations of antiquity. Noph (Memphis) was the ancient capital of lower Egypt, and No (Thebes) the capital of all Egypt. Their grandeur, especially the magnificent temples and images, was tremendous. Yet Jeremiah said, "Noph shall be waste and desolate without an inhabitant" (Jeremiah 46:19), and Ezekiel said, "No shall be rent asunder" (Ezekiel 30:16).

The prophecies were fulfilled centuries later. Of Egypt as a whole, it was said, "It shall be the basest of the kingdoms" (Ezekiel 29:15). Egypt continued as a great and powerful nation for many centuries after the prophecy was written, but finally it became a backward, impoverished, weak nation and has remained so ever since. It was not condemned to extinction, however, as were many other ancient nations. Actually, it is amazing that the most ancient of nations, Egypt, is still in existence after 4,000 years. Many Scriptures (for example, Isaiah 19:21–22) indicate prophetically that Egypt is still a nation in the last days.

Edom (Idumea) was a small but powerful nation descended from Esau. Its stronghold was in Mt. Seir, and its capital was Petra, the rock-walled city, impregnable as well as rich. Yet many prophecies had been uttered against it, and all have been fulfilled. Obadiah 18, for example, said, "There shall not be any remaining of the house of Esau; for the LORD hath spoken it."

Today, the Edomites are gone, without a trace. The same is true of the Philistines. Though Philistia continued to prosper until about A.D. 1200, Zephaniah had said, "The word of the LORD is against you; O Canaan, the land of the Philistines, I will even destroy thee, that there shall be no inhabitant" (Zephaniah 2:5). The Philistines have long since vanished.

What about Babylonia, the first great world empire? The Greek historian Herodotus had reported that Babylon was 15 miles square, surrounded by walls 350 feet high and 87 feet wide. Its avenues, parks, and public buildings were a beautiful sight to behold. Yet Jeremiah had prophesied, "The broad walls of Babylon shall be utterly broken, and her high gates shall be burned with fire" (Jeremiah 51:58). Many other like prophecies were directed against her, and eventually they came to pass.

The Assyrian Empire, with its great capital of Nineveh, was another colossus of antiquity. But God said, "He will stretch out His hand against the north, and destroy Assyria; and will make Nineveh a desolation, and dry like a wilderness" (Zephaniah 2:13). Nothing could have seemed more unlikely at the time Zephaniah wrote this, but it has been fully accomplished.

The two great cities of the Phoenicians were Tyre and Sidon. Of Tyre, God said, "They shall destroy the walls of Tyrus, and break down her towers: I will also scrape her dust from her, and make her like the top of a rock. It shall be a place for the spreading of nets in the midst of the sea" (Ezekiel 26:4–5).

Today, fishermen mend their nets on the barren rock where Tyre once stood. God also has said, in Ezekiel 26:14, "Thou shalt be built no more." The site of ancient Tyre is quite suitable for habitation, but the prophecy has stood fulfilled now for over 2,000 years, and Tyre has never been rebuilt.

Tyre's sister city, Sidon, was the object of a different type of prophecy. "For I will send into her pestilence, and blood into her streets; and the wounded shall be judged in the midst of her by the sword upon her on every side" (Ezekiel 28:23).

Sidon has continued to exist as a city even into the present, but she has suffered more warfare and bloodshed than almost any other city in history. Sidon has been destroyed and rebuilt many times and still exists today, in spite of all her suffering. Tyre, on the other hand, has never been rebuilt, thus confirming the prophecies.

Ashkelon was another great city, the birthplace of Herod the Great. It continued as a great city until finally destroyed in A.D. 1270. Long before, Zephaniah had prophesied, "Ashkelon [shall be] a desolation" (Zephaniah 2:4). The same prophecy had also warned of destruction upon two other Philistine cities, Ekron and Gaza. In both cases, the prophecy was fulfilled.

Similar judgments were forecast for Bethel (Amos 3:14–15), Samaria (Micah 1:6–7), Jericho (Joshua 6:26), and in the New Testament, for Capernaum, Bethsaida, and Chorazin (Malachi 11:20–23). All have been fulfilled as written.

Many other prophecies dealing with these and other nations have been fulfilled. There are also many other prophecies dealing with individual cities in the nations. Their fulfillment is a strong witness to divine inspiration.

II. The Sequence of Empires

A remarkable foreview of world history was given in Daniel 2, in the form of a dream that came to Nebuchadnezzar, king of Babylon. As interpreted by Daniel, the metallic image of the dream represented the entire subsequent course of world history, as influenced by four successive empires. Daniel's interpretation, as recorded in Daniel 2:37–45, indicated the first empire was the golden head of the image, Nebuchadnezzar's Babylonian Empire. The second would be the breast and arms of silver (fulfilled in the Medo-Persian Empire) and the third, the mid-section of brass (fulfilled in the Greek Empire of Alexander the Great). The fourth was the Roman Empire, represented by the iron legs, including the hips.

The order of metallic succession indicates both a successive decrease in value and a successive increase in strength. The decreasing value probably refers to the degree of personal control exercised by the emperor over the human and material resources of his kingdom, the increasing strength to the power of his armies and extent of his conquests.

The Roman Empire was not only the strongest of all but was to last the longest, as indicated by the greater lengths of the legs of the image. Its eventual twofold split into eastern and western divisions, with capitals at Rome and Constantinople, was pictured by the two legs. The break in continuity at the knees suggests the shift from political to religious unity of the two divisions, as maintained for so long by the Roman Catholic and Eastern Orthodox churches.

The Roman Empire did not persist indefinitely as a political unit, although it still does persist in the present east-west division of the heirs of the Roman Empire — western Europe and America in the west, and Russia, eastern Europe and the middle eastern states in the east. The legal systems, the educational systems, the military systems, the religious systems, and many other facets of modern society are direct descendants of Rome, still retaining the same spirit and much of the same form.

The feet, however, indicate a decided change in direction, and the mixture of iron and clay clearly speaks of the mixture of Roman-style imperialism with mass revolutionary movements. The final form of this succession is indicated by the ten toes representing ten kingdoms, five in the east and five in the west. These will be destroyed and superseded by the kingdom set up by Christ Himself over all the world when He returns.

This remarkable prophecy has been almost completely fulfilled. The sequence of world empires is now undoubtedly in the revolutionary "foot" stage, just before it finally assumes the "ten-toed" form prior to the establishment of Christ's kingdom.

While the great image prophesied the great sweep of empires throughout history, the prophecies given directly to Daniel himself, in the 8th and 11th chapters, forecast many of the specific details of the development of the Medo-Persian and Greek Empires, as well as numerous events that would take place in their contacts with Egypt, Syria, and Israel. The prophecies in these chapters are so numerous and so specific that they constitute the main reason why critics refuse to accept the authenticity of the Book of Daniel, insisting it must have been written after the events had taken place.

However, conservative scholars (for example, Dr. Robert Dick Wilson of Princeton University, in his classic *Studies in the Book of Daniel*) have thoroughly refuted all such critical arguments and confirmed the traditional date of authorship. The one and only reason today for questioning Daniel's genuineness any longer is the reluctance to believe in fulfilled prophecy. This, of course, is exactly the point. These prophecies confirm clearly and emphatically the fact of divine inspiration.

III. The Miracle of Israel

The continued existence of the Jews, after centuries of dispersal and persecution unique in human history, is a mute but eloquent testimony to fulfilled prophecy. The restoration of Israel as a nation among nations in modern times is merely the most recent in a long line of prophecies that deal with the Jewish people that have finally come to pass.

When the nation was first founded through Abraham, God promised, "I will make of thee a great nation . . . and I will bless them that bless thee, and curse him that curseth thee, and in thee shall all families of the earth be blessed" (Genesis 12:2–3).

Israel became a great nation under David and Solomon, and it is destined for even greater days in the future. The nations that have befriended the Jews (notably the United States and, to a lesser degree, England, France, and others) have indeed been blessed. Those that have persecuted the Jews (Egypt, Babylon, Assyria, Rome, Spain, Nazi Germany, and others) have eventually gone down to defeat and humiliation.

The seed of Abraham has indeed become a blessing to all families of the earth through the Holy Scriptures, almost all written by Jews, and through Jesus Christ. Some from every nation have found salvation and blessing through faith in Him.

God promised the children of Israel great blessing in the land of promise if they would remain faithful to Him. He also predicted great suffering, persecution, and worldwide dispersion when they forsook Him. These prophecies came to pass. Some of these warnings were as follows:

> The Lord shall scatter thee among all people, from the one end of the earth even unto the other. . . . And thy life shall hang in doubt before thee; and thou shalt fear day and night, and shalt have none assurance of thy life (Deuteronomy 28:64–66).

> And I will deliver them to be removed into all the kingdoms of the earth for their hurt, to be a reproach and a proverb, a taunt and a curse, in all places whither I shall drive them (Jeremiah 24:9).

My God will cast them away, because they did not
hearken unto him; and they shall be wanderers among
the nations (Hosea 9:17).

Numerous other such prophecies exist, concerning specific judgments and sufferings. But with all this, they would not be like so
many other nations of antiquity — indeed, like all other nations
who were driven from their homeland. "Though I make a full
end of all nations whither I have scattered thee, yet will I not
make a full end of thee" (Jeremiah 30:11).

It is humanly impossible that a nation could retain its identity without a homeland for 2,000 years; even more so that they
should then return and establish their ancient nation once again.
Yet this is exactly what the Bible had predicted.

Behold, I will take the children of Israel from among
the heathen, whither they be gone, and will gather them
on every side, and bring them into their own land (Ezekiel 37:21).

And it shall come to pass in that day, that the Lord
shall set His hand again the second time [note, the second
time — the first was when He brought them back from
the Babylonian captivity] to recover the remnant of His
people, which shall be left. . . . and shall assemble the outcasts of Israel, and gather together the dispersed of Judah
from the four corners of the earth (Isaiah 11:11–12).

The "wandering Jews" were without a national home for "many
days" (Hosea 3:4–5), and it seemed impossible that such prophecies as these could ever be fulfilled. Even many Bible-believing
Christians thought for centuries that God was through with
Israel and that all the Old Testament promises to Israel should
be spiritualized and applied to the church. But now, with the
return of the Jews and the re-establishment of their nation, it is
evident that God's Word means exactly what it says.

IV. Prophecies of the Last Days

In addition to the hundreds of biblical prophecies that have been fulfilled in the past, there is a special class of predictions that focus on the events of what the Scriptures call "the last days," the "latter times," or other similar expressions. In some cases, these expressions are used in a relative sense only, but usually they apply specifically to the closing days of the present age, days associated with the Second Coming of Christ to the earth.

Our purpose here is not to study eschatology, but rather to stress that these prophecies also provide further evidence of biblical inspiration, since many of them are being fulfilled today. In fact, as more and more of these ancient predictions are seen coming to pass, the evidence for the divine origin of the Bible is becoming stronger all the time.

We have already noted what is probably the most important of these end-time prophecies; namely, the re-establishment of Israel as a nation in its ancient homeland. It seems possible that a nation could be completely destroyed as an organized entity by an invading army (as Israel was by the Romans in A.D. 70), its people either slaughtered or scattered from one end of the world to the other, its land occupied and ruled by aliens for over 1,900 years, and yet survive as a distinct nationality, and then finally regain its homeland and be recognized as a viable nation once more by the other nations of the world. Yet it has happened in spite of the impossibilities, and to make it still more amazing, it was predicted many centuries before it happened.

The period known as "the times of the Gentiles" began when Israel, including Judah, first went into captivity in 588 B.C. Babylonia, Medo-Persia, Greece, and Rome were successive world empires, and their domain included the land of Israel. After Rome destroyed the city and the temple in A.D. 70 (as predicted by Christ Himself in Luke 19:41–44), the people of Israel were scattered "among all people, from the one end of the earth even unto the other" (Deuteronomy 28:64).

In this context, we come to a remarkable prophecy made by Jesus Christ: "And they shall fall by the edge of the sword, and shall be led away captive into all nations, and Jerusalem shall be trodden down of the Gentiles, until the times of the Gentiles be fulfilled" (Luke 21:24).

The word "fulfilled" is the same word in the Greek as "finished," and this prophecy clearly means the times of Gentile world-rule will be ended when Jerusalem is no longer under Gentile control. But this can only be accomplished when Christ returns to banish the Gentile nations from Jerusalem and to establish His own world-kingdom capital there. Thus, the restoration of Jerusalem to the chosen people is necessarily accompanied by the coming of their Messiah to reign there. This is also clearly indicated in Zechariah 12–14, as well as other Scriptures.

The Jews began to return to Palestine in small numbers in the early part of the 20th century, and then in much larger numbers after World War I and the Balfour Declaration. Jerusalem was still under British rule, however. After World War II, the Israeli nation declared its independence in 1948 and was soon recognized by most of the nations and by the United Nations. The new city of Jerusalem indeed did go back to the Jews at this time. However, the old city, including the all-important temple site on Mount Moriah, remained in the hands of the Jordanian Arabs.

In the "six-day war" of 1967, Israel finally recaptured even the old city of Jerusalem, and the Israelis insist they will never let it go again. At this writing, they have retained possession of all of Jerusalem for 37 long years, and there is no indication at all that the Arabs are going to recapture it.

Yet, the Lord has not come! The times of the Gentiles are still in full sway, even though Jerusalem has apparently gone back to the Jews.

There is one exception, however, and it makes all the difference, indicating with what fine lines the Holy Spirit inspires His Word. Jerusalem is not, in God's judgment, a collection of houses and streets, like other cities. It is a temple where God dwells, where His people approach Him through sacrifice, and where He meets with them.

As Solomon built the temple, God said, "I have chosen Jerusalem, that my name might be there" (2 Chronicles 6:6).

But long before this, God had first spoken through Moses, "There shall be a place which the Lord your God shall choose to cause his name to dwell there; thither shall ye bring all that I command you; your burnt offerings, and your sacrifices, your tithes, and the heave offering of your hand, and all your choice vows which ye vow unto the Lord" (Deuteronomy 12:11).

This place was not just any place in Jerusalem; it was an exact spot, chosen by God. It was on Mount Moriah (2 Chronicles 3:1), the spot that God told David to purchase from Ornan the Jebusite and to set up the altar there (1 Chronicles 21:18).

This was the same spot where Abraham had prepared to sacrifice his son Isaac almost a thousand years before (Genesis 22:2). It is only a short distance from Calvary itself.

This spot, to the Jews and to God, is Jerusalem. And amazingly, this one spot is the only spot in Jerusalem still controlled by Gentiles. It is on Mount Moriah that the Arabs have built their famous Dome-of-the-Rock, the second most holy place in the Muslim world. The Jews, for political or other reasons, have not yet dared to expel the Arabs from this site, raze it, and proceed to rebuild their temple, as they surely desire to do. It is apparently by this exceedingly slender thread, therefore, that the "times of the Gentiles" are still suspended. As the Lord Jesus said, "One jot or one tittle shall in no wise pass from the law, till all be fulfilled" (Matthew 5:18).

There are many other prophecies dealing with the alignment of the Gentile nations in the last days. The emergence of an alliance of Eastern European and Muslim nations under the leadership and domination of Russia, all arrayed in opposition to Israel and the Western nations, is prophesied in Ezekiel 38:1–16.

The rise of a vast oriental confederacy of nations is described in Revelation 16:12.

The development of a European union of nations comparable to the ancient Roman Empire is suggested in Daniel 7:19–24 and other passages.

In response to the question, "What shall be the sign of thy coming, and of the end of the world?" the Lord Jesus answered, "Nation shall rise against nation, and kingdom against kingdom: and there shall be famines, and pestilences, and earthquakes, in divers places. All these are the beginning of sorrows" (or, more accurately, "the first birth pains") (Matthew 24:3). The Hebrew idiom conveys the thought of a worldwide state of war. Thus, the prophetic sign entails a world war, accompanied by great physical calamities, as the initial sign that a new world is about to be born. This was clearly fulfilled in the decade from 1914 to 1924, when the first world war took place, followed by the world's greatest pestilence (the influenza epidemic of 1918), the world's greatest famine (leading to the starvation of hundreds of millions, especially in Russia and China, after the war and the communist revolution), and the world's most calamitous earthquakes (in China in 1920 and Japan in 1923), all took place. The world since that time has continued to experience these "birth pains," with World War II, the Cold War, great numbers of local wars, the Great Depression, continued deadly earthquakes, epidemics of polio, cholera, AIDS, and other diseases, and innumerable other "troubles" (Mark 13:8).

A fulfilled prophecy of an entirely different sort is found in 2 Peter 3:3–4. "There shall come in the last days scoffers . . . saying . . . all things continue as they were from the beginning of the creation."

This is the doctrine of *evolutionary uniformitarianism*, which professes to explain the origin and development of all things in terms of the uniform operation of the same natural laws and processes, which still "continue" today. The rise of this dogma took place in the 19th century, and has for a hundred years been the basic philosophy of the educational and scientific establishments. There was no way that Peter could have foreseen this development, 1,800 years in the future, apart from divine inspiration.

In relation to the realm of science and education, it was prophesied in Daniel that, at "the time of the end: many shall run to and fro, and knowledge shall be increased" (Daniel 12:4). The Hebrew words imply a vast increase in both frequency and speed of travel, as well as other forms of communication, along with great advances in science and technology.

Conflict in the economic and social realms in the last days is forecast in James 5:1–6. For ages, in all nations, the poor have been exploited by the rich, and the working classes by the privileged classes.

The uprising of the laborers in the latter days, leading to a "day of slaughter," is not only specifically predicted by James, and also implied in Daniel 2:41–43, Revelation 18:1–19, and other passages.

These prophecies have been fulfilled in part, first in the French revolution, later in the Russian revolution and other communist-led upheavals. More is undoubtedly yet to come, especially when the ill-fed, poorly housed masses of the world come to realize that even their own revolutionary movements are financed and controlled in large measure by those "kings and merchants of the earth" who traffic in the "souls of men."

Moral conditions of the last days are prophesied to descend into the degradation of the "days of Noah" (Luke 17:26). But perhaps the most striking prediction associated with moral conditions in the last days is that the characteristics of professing religious people, in the realm of Christendom, will be essentially the same as those of the heathen in the old pagan world. That is, the catalog of the sins of those in the last days who have "a form of godliness" (2 Titus 3:1–7, especially verse 5), is practically identical with that of the ancient godless rebels of Romans 1:28–31.

Again, it seems impossible that Paul could have anticipated such a strange, sad development except by inspiration.

Religious apostasy in the ranks of professed Christian leaders is also prophesied in other Scriptures. False teachers will deny the second coming of Christ (2 Peter 3:3), and they will even deny "the Lord that bought them" (2 Peter 2:1). They will still never come "to the knowledge of the truth" (2 Timothy 3:7), despite much education ("ever learning"), and they will even "turn away their ears from the truth, and shall be turned unto fables" (2 Timothy 4:4). All of these prophecies are being fulfilled today throughout the "Christian" world.

A particularly ominous form of apostasy is to be found in the rapid rise of demonism in the last days. "In the latter times, some shall depart from the faith, giving heed to seducing spirits, and doctrines of [demons]" (1 Timothy 4:1). Jesus said, "There shall arise false Christs, and false prophets, and shall shew great signs and wonders" (Matthew 24:24). During the great tribulation period of the last days, these trends will culminate in a worldwide return to Satan worship (Revelation 13:4, 8). Before that, they will "worship [demons], and idols" (Revelation 9:20) and do so especially in connection with the use of drugs (the word "sorceries," in Revelation 9:21, is a Greek word from which we actually transliterate our English word "pharmaceutical," and means "magical incantations by the ritual use of drugs").

The amazing upsurge of spiritism, astrology, witchcraft, and Satanism all over the world in the past few years, along with the tremendous increase of drug use, especially by young people, certainly is an ominous sign of the imminent advent of Antichrist, but at the same time is a striking fulfillment of prophecy. It would seem paradoxical that an age of scientific enlightenment could be followed so quickly by a widespread revival of paganism and occultism, but that is exactly what has happened, just as the Bible predicted.

We have only scratched the surface. There are scores of other biblical prophecies that have already been fulfilled or are presently in process of fulfillment. There is no other book like the Bible.

> For the prophecy came not in old time by the will of man; but holy men of God spake as they were moved by the Holy Ghost (2 Peter 1:21).[1]

---

1. *The Henry M. Morris Study Bible* (Green Forest, AR: Master Books, 2012), appendix 13, largely taken from Henry Morris, *Many Infallible Proofs* (Green Forest, AR: Master Books, 1996), p. 189–203.

Appendix IV

Use of "Palestine" versus "Israel"

One of the most important ongoing hot button geopolitical issues today has to do with who owns the land of Israel. This issue remains a stumbling block to the governments of the world and seems to be impossible to resolve. The Israeli people continue to claim the land based on the accuracy of the Word of God and the promises contained within granting this land to them by God Himself (see Genesis chapter 15). The Palestinian leadership on the other hand, has repeatedly sought to legitimize their right to the land, claiming it belongs to them and not the Jews. One of their BIG lies is that the land was always referred to as Palestine. Historically, this is inaccurate! There has never been a Palestinian state in the history of the world. Therefore, when I pick up Bible after Bible, and read in introductions to books as well as maps, and see Israel referred to as Palestine or Palestina, I am shocked.

Allow me to cite examples. The New American Standard, 1977 edition published by AMG of Chattanooga, TN, in the introduction to Mark cites the book was written, *"for the benefit of those who lived outside **Palestine**."* The same intro states, *the book was probably written about 67–68 a.d.* Further, imagine my shock to read Exodus 15:14 in the Cambridge University Press, King James Wide Margin Edition, where it states: *"The people shall hear, and be afraid: sorrow shall take hold on the inhabitants of **Palestina**."* Joel 3:4 states, *"Yea, and what have ye to do with me, O Tyre, and Zidon, and all the coasts of **Palestine?**"*

These are all erroneous translations of the Hebrew word *Pelesheth* and always refer to the Philistines. The fact is, there was NO Palestine, as this land was called Israel from the time of Jacob until A.D. 135. The Roman Emperor Hadrian, following the second Jewish revolt led by Simon Bar Kochba, changed the name of Israel to Syria Palestina which he took from the Hebrew word *Pelesheth*, which we know as Philistia. Why? Because the Jews hated the Philistines and this was a slap in the face to them! This was the ultimate insult! The land of Israel was comprised of Galilee, Samaria, Judea, and Philistia. Philistia was the land of the archenemies of Israel, the Philistines. The Philistines were not Arab but European, and came from the Island of Crete. They occupied five cities along the western part of Israel: Ashdod, Ashkelon, Ekron, Gath, and Gaza. Therefore to refer to Israel as Palestine anytime before A.D. 135 is historically inaccurate and provides credibility to a lie.

Was the word ever used before A.D. 135? Yes, that is the word *Philistia* was used by Herodotus (considered by many to be the father of ancient history as well as the father of lies) in the 5th century B.C. When his works were translated into English they did so as *Palestine*. Wrong! Josephus, in his Jewish Wars, also makes one reference to Philistia translated again as Palestine. Wrong! Other than these two examples, I cannot discover any other source citing Israel as Palestine prior to 135. Jesus however refers to *Israel* numerous times in the Gospels and never uses the word *Philistia*. When Titus destroyed the Temple in A.D. 70, the Roman government minted a coin that read *Judea Capta* or Judea Captive, meaning Judea was captured! If it had been Philistia or Palestina it would have been stated as such.

The *Believer's Study Bible*, 1991, published by Nelson, continues the big lie where in the Index to Maps it lists the following: "Map 6. Palestine in Christ's Time." I understand that the majority of the Bible maps used today actually come from the time of the British Mandate from 1917–1948. It is true that the land was called Palestine since 135, but this is the 21st century and in light of the political issue we need to update the information. There are many other examples I could cite as this appears to be fairly common.

So, why the issue — what difference does it make? It makes a difference because it legitimizes the false claims the government, the media, and the haters of Israel propagate concerning the Jewish right to live in the land God gave them. It gives the false impression that there was a Land of Palestine in ancient times and perpetuates the lie that the Jews took away the Palestinians land. The United Nations has recognized a Palestinian state and even gone so far as to recognize Mahmoud Abbas as its president. This is yet another example of the U.N.'s historical and biased ignorance. If truth matters, this matters! Bible publishers of the Holy Word of God need to get it right. If this is due to erroneous information or simple oversight, then fix it! If it is due to tolerance and so-called political correctness, then fix it! History is on the side of Israel and the Word of God![1]

---

1. See more at http://discoverymissions.blogspot.com/2014/03/an-open-letter-to-bible-publishers.html.

Appendix V
Understanding the Balfour Declaration

The famed Balfour Declaration issued on November 2, 1917, was a huge step as God once again continued what seemed to be a painstakingly slow process in setting the world stage for the re-gathering of the Jewish people to their land. The Ottoman Turkish empire had risen to dominate the land now known as Palestine in the year 1514 and would remain in power some 400 years until their demise at the end of World War 1 in 1914. The Turks, while they are of the Muslim religion are not Arab, and were a brutal people. These oppressors did not care about the land nor those living in it beyond the revenue they could collect and the power they could wield.

The back story on this amazing declaration is that in the midst of the war the British ran into a problem. The problem was that Germany, their enemy, had cornered the market on the production of a necessary component of arms production — acetone. Acetone is necessary to produce cordite, which is a powerful propellant explosive that allows the firing of ammunition without generating telltale smoke giving away one's position. This shortage of acetone was greatly hampering Britain's war effort. Enter a Jewish scientist by the name of Chaim Weizmann. Weizmann

Foreign Office,
November 2nd, 1917.

Dear Lord Rothschild,

I have much pleasure in conveying to you, on behalf of His Majesty's Government, the following declaration of sympathy with Jewish Zionist aspirations which has been submitted to, and approved by, the Cabinet.

"His Majesty's Government view with favour the establishment in Palestine of a national home for the Jewish people, and will use their best endeavours to facilitate the achievement of this object, it being clearly understood that nothing shall be done which may prejudice the civil and religious rights of existing non-Jewish communities in Palestine, or the rights and political status enjoyed by Jews in any other country".

I should be grateful if you would bring this declaration to the knowledge of the Zionist Federation.

The famous Balfour Declaration of 1917

invented a process to synthesize acetone via fermentation. David Lloyd-George, minister of munitions during the war who would become prime minister of Britain following the war, learned of Weizmann's invention and was a supporter of the Zionist movement that had begun in 1897. David Lloyd-George supported the idea of Zionism in that a return to the land by Jews would help facilitate and secure the post-war control of Palestine by the British.

Wikipedia adds some interesting facts:

> David Lloyd George, who was Prime Minister at the time of the Balfour Declaration, told the Palestine Royal Commission in 1937 that the Declaration was made "due to propagandist reasons." Citing the position of the Allied and Associated Powers in the ongoing war, Lloyd George said, in the Report's words, "In this critical situation it was believed that Jewish sympathy or the reverse would make a substantial difference one way or the other to the Allied cause. In particular Jewish sympathy would confirm the support of American Jewry, and would make it more difficult for Germany to reduce her military commitments and improve her economic position on the eastern front." Lloyd George then said:

> > The Zionist leaders gave us a definite promise that, if the Allies committed themselves to giving facilities for the establishment of a national home for the Jews in Palestine, they would do their best to rally Jewish sentiment and support throughout the world to the Allied cause. They kept their word.[1]

In other words, the Jews had performed as requested and therefore to show good faith they honored the request of Weizmann for the recognition of a Jewish homeland and proceeded to issue

---

1. https://en.wikipedia.org/wiki/Balfour_Declaration; Palestine Royal Commission Report, Cmd 5479, 1937, p. 23–24.

the declaration. I should point out that the wording of the declaration was chosen very carefully and by intent was ambiguous.

For example, the phrase "Jewish homeland" carried no legal value, whereas, had it read "Jewish State" it clearly would have. The phrase "in Palestine" as opposed to simply "of Palestine," was purposeful as well. Therefore, the phrase "the establishment in Palestine of a National Home for the Jewish people" was intended and understood by all concerned to mean at the time of the Balfour Declaration that Palestine would ultimately become a "Jewish Commonwealth" or a "Jewish State," if only Jews came and settled there in sufficient numbers.

In spite of the ambiguity of the declaration it was, in fact, the very first time in 1,900 years that a major national entity gave credence to the idea of a Jewish homeland. Although this would not become a reality until 1948, the plan was creeping forward and God was doing His work, in His way, and according to His time.

Appendix VI
The Time of Israel's Judgment

Most conservative scholars believe the re-gathering of the Jews to their land on May 14, 1948, was the most significant biblical and historical event since the Resurrection of Jesus Christ. Further, they, for the most part, agree that the event marked the beginning of the "terminal generation." I happen to agree.

Please allow me to explain and demonstrate. The key to understanding that God's judgment upon Israel's sin is temporary and not eternal is found in an obscure passage of scripture in the Old Testament, Ezekiel 4:4–6:

> Then lie on your left side and put the sin of the people of Israel upon yourself. You are to bear their sin for the number of days you lie on your side. I have assigned you the same number of days as the years of their sin. So for 390 days you will bear the sin of the people of Israel.
>
> After you have finished this, lie down again, this time on your right side, and bear the sin of the people of Judah. I have assigned you 40 days, a day for each year (NIV).

We must remember there were 12 united tribes of Israel under the kings Saul, David, and Solomon. However, upon Solomon's death, the tribes were divided with 10 tribes in the north with their capital at Samaria, and from then on they were referred to as Israel. The 2 tribes of Benjamin and Judah continued with their capital at Jerusalem and were known simply as Judah. Therefore, when reading the Old Testament, we must keep in mind who is being spoken of in the historical narrative.

Israel has so sinned against God with their long list of bad kings that God serves them with a sentence of 390 years of sin debt.

Judah, on the other hand, was given 40 years of sin debt.

Combining the two we find the collective sin debt becomes 430 years total.

We know the last king of Israel was Hoshea and in 722 b.c. the Assyrians, under the leadership of Sargon II, son of Shalmaneser, attacked the 10 northern tribes and deported the people to Halah and Habor on the Gozan River and in some of the cities of the Medes.[1] We have no historical nor biblical record of their return. However, they no doubt did return at some point in small groups of families.

We further know that King Nebuchadnezzar of Babylon invaded Judah on three separate occasions, and the Temple of Solomon was desecrated and destroyed in 586 b.c. and King Zedekiah was captured, blinded, and taken to Babylon.

So let's think through this history. Let's take the 430 years of combined sin debt owed to God and subtract the 70 years served in Babylon (605–536) and we are left with 360 years. Let's then take the 360 years and apply a principle taught in Leviticus 26 where we learn that God warned four times that if they did not turn from their sin and repent God would multiply their sin seven-fold.

---

1. Ed Hindson and Gary Yates, *Essence of the Old Testament: A Survey* (Nashville, TN: B & H Publishing Group, 2012), p. 184.

So, did they repent? If you read Nehemiah 2–6 and Ezra, we must say NO! — 360 x 7= 2,520 years of sin debt. The Jews use a lunar calendar of 30 days per month or 360 days per year. Therefore 2,520 years x 360 days per year = 907,200 days of debt.

We then divide the 907,200 days by the Gregorian calendar in use today consisting of 365.2425 days per year and we arrive at 2,483 years and 8 months of debt. By subtracting the year and month of Judah's return from Babylon, namely 536 and the third month, and remembering there is no such thing as the year zero, the number we get is 1948 and the fifth month.

This is the very month and year Israel became a nation once again, and the terminal generation began. Question: how long is a generation? Some have taught it is 40 years, others 70, but what does the Bible say? The answer is found in Genesis 15 verses 13 and 16. It is 100 years! Jesus is coming soon, and the most important indicator is the return of Israel to their God-given land.

Are We Living in the Last Days?

" Prophecy fulfillment, especially in our time, could be one of the most effective witnessing tools available to us.
- **Gary Frazier**

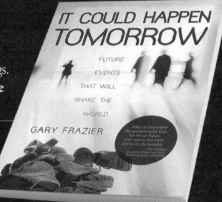

IT COULD HAPPEN TOMORROW

FUTURE EVENTS THAT WILL SHAKE THE WORLD

GARY FRAZIER

A book of warnings.
**A message of hope
for tomorrow.**

$12.99 | 978-0-89221-711-3

New Leaf Press
A Division of New Leaf Publishing Group

Buy Today At NLPG.com

According to the results of recent surveys, Americans overwhelmingly believe that HEAVEN exists, though a much smaller number believe that HELL exists.

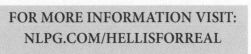

This is WHY it matters!

What if those who do not believe in Hell die one day and find they made a tragic and eternal mistake? *Hell is for Real* is a clear search for truth. Truth matters for the simple reason that we all have a divine appointment with death. The good news is there is a source that provides answers for each and every one who cares to seek the truth. Join the search and choose wisely because eternity is too long to be wrong.

$12.99 | 978-0-89221-732-8
Paper | 160 pages

FOR MORE INFORMATION VISIT:
NLPG.COM/HELLISFORREAL

New Leaf Press
A Division of New Leaf Publishing Group
www.newleafpress.net

For years, both on my show and now working with Christians United for Israel, I've seen firsthand the miraculous nature of the modern nation of Israel. Often, though, I find that people don't have basic information about its history and current place on the prophetic timeline. Jim and Gary have managed that in a big way in *Miracle of Israel*, which comes along at the perfect time. I highly recommend this book, whether you want to introduce it to your church, family, or a secular friend.

> **Erick Stakelbeck, Host, "The Watchman" show on TBN, Director, Christians United for Israel's Watchman Project**

Our churches are now silent on this topic. Were it not for a few ministries and authors, no one would know this vital information. I am thankful that Gary Frazier and Jim Fletcher have brought these timeless truths back to the forefront.

> **Jan Markell**
> **Olive Tree Ministries**